M A R   v v

of

M Y S T E R Y

IMAGE

I remember bone marrow that my Nana used to dig out after boiling and cooking for hours in a big pot on the back of the stove. It was soft and she spread it on thick pieces of dark bread. It was luscious, rich, soaking into the bread. Marrow bones—a treat on certain Sundays, visits to her house. The connection to liturgy—the Word, Scriptures spread on bread—bone marrow of the spirit spread thickly on the bread of justice, the bread of hope to feed the poor, the little ones that need nourishment and strength more than the others—that is good news to the poor, the liturgy of word and bread. Nana feeding her grandchildren, Grandfather God feeding his little ones, us.

MARROW
of
MYSTERY

———— ✳ ————

Selected Poems

Megan McKenna

SHEED & WARD
Franklin, Wisconsin

As an apostolate of the Priests of the Sacred Heart, a
Catholic religious congregation, the mission of Sheed &
Ward is to publish books of contemporary impact and
enduring merit in Catholic Christian thought and action.
The books published, however, reflect the opinions of their
authors and are not meant to represent the official position
of the Priests of the Sacred Heart.

2001

Sheed & Ward
7373 South Lovers Lane Road
Franklin, Wisconsin 53132
1-800-266-5564

Cover design by Robin Booth
Cover art: Wall painting from Villa of Livia, in Prima Porta
near Rome, late first century A.D. Painted in the fresco
technique.
Interior design by GrafixStudio, Inc.

Library of Congress Cataloging-in-Publication Data

McKenna, Megan.
    Marrow of mystery : selected poems / Megan McKenna.
      p. cm.
    ISBN 1-58051-092-2 (alk.paper)
      1. Christian poetry, American. I. Title.

PS3563.C3753 M3 2001
811'.54--dc21   00-053142

For dear Nena,
who walked me through the doorway of Asia

And for Sue and Doug,
who sent me off with lifelines

CONTENTS

INTRODUCTION

When I was young, my brothers and sisters and I would all converge on our Nana's apartment in New York. It was a Sunday noon ritual after church. We crowded around her table. The treat was always the same: hot boiled marrow bones specially requested from the butcher down the block. The smell hit you as the front door was opened. Sweet and strong, but basically indescribable. Great slices of dark bread nice and warm lay waiting on the table.

Standing in her apron, her white hair pulled back in a bun, Nana would eye us each in turn and fish the marrow bones out of the steaming pot onto a plate. Then she would scoop out the insides. They looked gross, awful, and ugly. She would smear them, slather them, on the bread. Each of us would be served and immediately we would bite into our bread, running our tongues over the marrow. But always, the youngest or anyone sickly or weak, would get served first and got the biggest bones and the most marrow. We never spoke, only smelled and sniffed and sighed and made slurping noises as we ate.

I could never put together something that smelled and tasted that good with what looked so icky and awful and came out of bones. We ate the insides of bones! But I learned early about many mysteries around that table. Silence is the appropriate response to such goodness—no talk after eating. What is ugly can belie appearances, give meaning, and take you places you never dreamed was hidden there. Marrow was meant to be shared—but first it was to be given to the weakest, the youngest, and those most in need of such infusions of life. And there are rituals that make religion meaningful. Being the one who ladled out the goodness and spread it around meant that you didn't eat yourself, but my Nana never seemed to mind much. Her delight was in watching us eat.

But what has stayed with me most is: mystery has to be dug out of bones, looks ugly, tastes luscious, but really is indescribable—beyond words—but oh, the sheer delight in digging and smearing and letting others feast on it.

These poems could be called autobiographical, and some are, but many are more to the heart of just being human and having either stumbled into the marrow of life or been handed outright, for no reason at all, a piece of thick homemade bread smeared with the marrow of mystery by so many generous folk.

I travel ten, eleven months of the year—to Asia, islands galore, Canada, the South China seas, Celtic green dollops in an ocean of blue, the United States, and Latin America. I crisscross earth going backwards and forwards in time and place. It is exhausting and exhilarating and, although I usually go as the teacher or the preacher or the storyteller, I am always the one taught, caught up in wisdom, and called to radical altering of my life and thoughts.

But I always come back—back home—a place of wild light, a small place in northern New Mexico—a place of high sky, enchanted mesas, and blood-of-Christ mountains, to a land close by wilderness. And that wildness strays often into my path and backyard, and I lie in wait for it. It feeds me more than anything else, even more than words and music: it is silence, solitude, loneliness loved, wildness visited—in hawk's eye, wolf's howl, raptor and reptile and skunk, and the way land, sky, and weather all come together. It seeps into me and I need it as though I need a transfusion. That is why there are so many poems that are triggered by storms, lack of rain, seasons shifting, and places apart from usual human habitation. I cannot stay away too long from places off the beaten path. If I can't get home, then I must go off into the unknown wherever I am traveling.

After months on the road, coping with 40 degrees Celsius and monsoon rains, sitting on runways delayed, days of gray cold, hordes of people, words, and translations—and being a stranger, a visitor, a foreigner, a guest—I have to come back to being a monk, a hermit outwardly for a while since I am really always that internally. And in those travels there is violence, haste, ignorance, injustice, horror, betrayals, as well as enduring graces, faithfulness in the face of brutality, snippets of unrepeatable glory, ordinary courtesies, and gross inequities. Billions of human beings brushing shoulders, caressing one another, and shoving one another aside must be absorbed somehow. It's osmosis—and after such dense periods of absorption, there has to be utter silence, a time to brush all spirits, words, and presences away from one's heart as an old native elder showed me with his dance of hands. It has to be done periodically outside, literally, with the earth and the sky and the waters as witnesses and, in lieu of that, in pockets of solitude, gleaned moments of sanctuary, and more often than not, in words—poems, pieces of stories, images given, memories put on a page, soul and mind emptied out.

These pieces are culled from stacks of journals, reams of attempts and poems just given fully formed. Some of the poems merited titles, some did not. They are bits and pieces, scooped out of bones—the marrow of life's richness found in every human being and all over earth in remnants, ruins, and all that shares this place with us—the beasts and the birds, spirits and schools of fish, light and weather patterns, and the ground itself. All talks. I seek to listen. And sometimes poetry is the residue of the conversations, more often of prayer, of conscious remembering, of the struggle to make meaning or to brush away accumulation of spirit, to empty the pockets of soul. This sort of writing, reflection, and communion is the undercurrent, the daily stuff of life, running under and through the books, the talks, the preaching, and the storytelling. It's just pieces of marrow bones spread on bread. It has nourished me but it must be shared out for mystery speaks most surely in silences shared and when the marrow is dug out, spread on bread—or scrawled on a page. Some of the digging has been done, but the feast is always laid out before us. This book is really just a pot of marrow bones reeking of mystery, given as a gift.

INCARNATIONS

The original Incarnation was God giving form and face to creation, making a place outside, a place other than just God. The Jewish mystics believe God made a space, breathed out, whispered, sighed a sound—and the Mysterious Holy One set in motion all that is and has ever been and will be still.

And Christians believe fervently that after eons of waiting and waiting, God spoke, sighed, and dared a Word that had been there from the beginning, and the Word was God and that Word took on flesh and blood and bone and mind and made earth his dwelling place. This Word has stayed on with us and will until forever, lingering in the absent presence of the Spirit.

Once the Word became flesh. Now all flesh seeks to become word, to transpose the mystery. We are made in the image and likeness of God. Our flesh speaks, sings, weeps, stutters, and gasps as we make meaning with our lives.

There are persons who are clear phrases, a word carefully pronounced, articulating small pieces of mystery. There are people, moments that incarnate a truth, pose a question, blurt out unselfconsciously a wild proposition that is hinged to the Holy and the doors swing wide. These poems seek to remember, to put on paper these incarnations of God walking earth on clay feet, with shining eyes and gestures of radiant clarity. They live and breathe and exhale some detail of Mystery's transcendence through the marrow of our bones.

ELEGY FOR LOUIS
(Thomas Merton)

Twenty-nine years have gone by.
It was a cold gray morning.
In the early dark the radio punctured restless sleep.
5 A.M. New York City, 23rd Street and 7th Avenue,
an apartment across the street from the Chelsea Hotel,
next door to the YMCA. A dump of an efficiency.
Home that year, 1968, teaching uptown in Harlem.

The news came on. Eyes still closed.
Last item—Bangkok, Thailand.
The infamous monk Thomas Merton
was bizarrely electrocuted in a hotel room.
He was coming home from Asia in a military transport,
sealed in a coffin—to Gethsemane. The irony
was not lost on the commentator:
This man had protested that war from the hills
        of Kentucky battling with words,
hunkered down and holding out alone
        on a grassy knoll.

I kept my eyes closed.
This was too much reality to grasp in
the shadows of another day. The names
rose like warm blood in my throat:
JFK, RFK, MLK, now another: TM
or Father Louis, as he was known.
He was dead. I awoke, weeping.

(continued)

We've learned to live 29 years without him.
But wonder what we would have become if
he were here today? Joy to you, Louie:
Remember us in your delight face to face!
It was the beginning of wisdom rooted in wood:
the cross contemplating pain, a long loving hard
look at what's grindingly hard to see.
His death: a new seed of contemplation.
                              —*December 10, 1998*

Night drifting under a cold moon.
Pieces of memory read somewhere long ago—
of a cold mountain crazy man Han-shan.
I smile as the image rises in my watching mind.
He would scribble a poem a *gatha* on tree bark
and drop it thoughtlessly on a path.
If he was seen, even for a moment, he would run
and disappear into one of his caves—and it
would obligingly close up behind him.
Wow! Talk about protecting one's solitude.
        (Protective custody?)
Tonight, hounded by people, I'm jealous
of Han-shan and his wild antics,
his mountain fastness and his ease
in disappearing right before your eyes.
When pursued he left, scattering bits of his presence
        in bare trees.
For a few moments moon and I,
we cast a cold eye on each other
and our faces bear reflecting cold smiles!
Time to go inside and cradle a cup
        of bitter hot tea.

A BLESSING

The man was tired
From practicing being a pilgrim, pack on his back
Fourteen and a half miles buffeted by wind, baked by sun.
Soon Compostella, Santiago in a field of stars.
He gestured and said: maybe I've showed you already.
This is the sign I love (in the language of the deaf he was
often wont to speak)
A hand passed down across his face, fingers flew from his
mouth
Skyward.
He spoke without words: Holy Spirit.
I sat across the room, stunned
For an instant I had seen the Holy veiled, revealed,
Shining breath expelled, flung from his mouth
With lightness and wild abandon,
Freedom and reverence turned to awe and envy
At such profligate giving and offhanded ease.
A question arose in the silence:
Does glory ever show, ever slip loose or startle another like
that in me?
Oh God. May it be so. Amen. Amen. Amen.
Breathe.

—Speke, England

Good Friday. Outdoor stations with the youth group.
Windy almost spring day but grey. Mary wore black biker
shorts and tennis shoes, wrapping a piece of sky-blue cloth
around her sometimes. It fell to her knees. She kept tossing
her long, curly, brown-red hair back and forth then
remembered to put the veil back on again. I watched from a
distance as they read their lines. I tried to believe that it was
for more than show. Mostly it looked sad and a bit
ludicrous. Then I watched the others. They prayed and
didn't seem bothered by the flighty Mary. She was one of
theirs. They had known her all along. And then I smiled
and remembered ruefully. It was April Fools Day too.

People so long hungry for dignity and freedom
and so long starved that their memory only lives
and sparks sometimes in their eyes.
Music, the digereedoo knows
and the one who blows and the one who hears
find their hearts beating faster,
their limbs jerking, their bodies once again—
reaching—so they dance and come together
feeding on the longing shared.
Mostly it's a night feast
And there are fires and dry cracked earth
And many eyes wild and knowing watching
beyond the rim of guests and spectators.
The stars witness. Tomorrow—they all know—
Again the hunger pains will be a little more unbearable,
sharper but even the footprinted dusty earth will be a place
that you can enter when you need the hope more
than you need anything else.

—Australia

RAVEN-PROPHET

The prophet commanded to hide with the ravens at the
Wadi. Daily they arrive, punctual as dawn and dusk to feed
him meat and bread until the waters dry up. Commanded
next to find the widow at Zarephath—God having
commended Elijah to her care. First a request for water.
Then flour cakes and oil made from the last bit of stored
provisions. Meal to welcome starvation's slow death,
transformed into continual communion.
Trinity: ragged prophet begging alms of a widow woman
and her young son. She obeys—first a stranger's request for
a drink, then more, daily bread, then hospitality—an upper
room of his own. And then the child dies as she holds him
in her lap, ancient form of pieta. She is stricken by guilt but
the prophet sees—not her sin but her faithfulness and
knows all the land is struggling under the heavy hand of
Yahweh who can no longer ignore the brutal widespread
lack of justice, and so, of any worship.

Elijah takes the child up to his room near the sky, lays him
tenderly on the bed and cries to Yahweh to see clearly one
woman's kindness to him albeit obedience to true laws of
stranger care-taking. He lies stretched out along the child's
body, manprophet, innocent boy, sharing breath and air of
Yahweh and God hears his obedient one's stubborn, rude
prayer. The air wavers, the heart stirs. The child revives.
Elijah carries the boy back down the stairs and gives him
back to his mother. He stays on as guest but now she knows
what all Israel will soon have to bear: the Word of the Lord
dwells in his mouth, life-giving and death-defying—and so
death dealing, too. The underside of the prophet is healer
and the one who brings back from the dead with his blunt
truth-telling learned from Yahweh, used on his people and
turned again on God. God loves such consistency in his
friends.

(continued)

Soon afterwards, the prophet will be commanded again—to attack the city with searing words and the presence of the true God seeking his own gone off apart. He will obey and get carried away slaughtering all four hundred false prophets of the Queen. And he will run again to the mountain fastness to try and find God—in thunder, in lightening, in earthquake and instead be attacked by a whisper of wind. He will hide his face from such tenderness and closeness—God's breath on his face, drawing near to kiss him on his mouth—giving life, returning his favor showed to widow's child.

It seems prophets, too, must learn the ways of God—to hide out with ravens, widows, whispers—all intimate nearness of the One God's truth-telling presence—the violence is to be against death, against injustice, against faithlessness, against lies, and resistance is found in solitariness, in water and begging and the company of widows, winged ones and whispers of wind—God's nonviolent dwelling place and hidden visits among us—Knowing this it's not strange that another prophet, at ease in canyon deserts and alone at night prayers will stop the crying and death of the poor and give the widow of Naim back her son and give his life breath to tell us all the truth of how near Yahweh has wanted to come to us.

Incarnation—God's merciful breath in our faces, our mouths, our ears, still the Spirit of God, the Word of truth that kills and brings life as fiercely as any sword, as daily as bread from ravens and as humbly as whispers that make us hide our faces. The dwelling places where God chooses to hide out: Wadi and raven abode, widow's hospitality; mountain winds, cave—that reveal God's pleasure, substance, truthfulness and nonviolent, death defiance and kiss of life, begging us to obey today.

My next door neighbor is old. Eighty old. She gets around. Slow. Plodding tho not like a tortoise. Reed thin in any weather or wind. Sometimes she sits on the porch in an old faded lawn chair that sags even with her small frame. I thought she watched the birds but when I approached her quietly, she's staring, not really there. I wonder where she goes. In those moments, she's an old bent fence, a sagging long-unused clothes line.

She saw me looking for feathers one evening and next day she waited for me to come home, her hands full of dove and pigeons leavings. I was so touched, so torn. She is so lonely, so eager for companionship. Now I try to make time, spend time. We stand in the grass, and for awhile her eyes light up and she becomes animated, talkative, inquisitive. I find she's lived there for twelve years. Just a retired teacher, not much left around her. Never been inside her apt. She's even afraid of the raccoon and skunk that come from beyond the fence in the high overgrown grasses. She's desperately searching for home base—someone to know on a daily basis.

I come and go so much. I'm not good company or reliable. I see her sometimes from my second-story window while I'm working at the computer. She is down below with the birdseed, looking for feathers, and I don't have the heart to tell her—anything but the doves and pigeons. Her eyes can only see those in the grass. I take her offerings, gratefully and hide them, to take them out in the garbage. She is so fragile and so endearing and so sad and so still alive, like a bird, one of many pigeons or doves, unnoticed, forgotten, unappreciated, left over, fringe nested, and so precious and to be cared for, like the lilies of the field and the birds of the air.

Do you know that I stand only a hair's breath from you—
conscious of smell, tingling of flesh, aware of even your
    breathing
tasting every bite of your silence. That I love you, knowing
    you not.
There is between us a gulf, a grand canyon that I cannot
    cross.
You stand aware of me, knowing all my desire, longing
    need, wanting
it to grow, consume me while I yet wait on your word,
    gesture, turning glance.
There are some things that cannot be acted upon or done.
    They must be given,
gifted since there is no power left, except sheer mercy,
    being chosen, being held,
and taken to be kept. I will not refuse you this joy—the joy
    of one wanting you.
I know. It has taken me near half a century to learn this
    wisdom. You know
how painful it is to be so near, untouchable, bound to wait
    upon another's word
or pleasure, learning obedience that crosses out all other
    sense of purpose, meaning—
hope? Yes, you know—once humanness held your flesh and
    your spirit and you
learned it through suffering. You let me wait. It is your love's
    first grace,
carving out a place inside that later can be filled. Eternity
    stretches lazily near.
It is not pity I await but recognition and communion, even
    as I know that that one
moment will take my life forever. It is that killing moment
    that I know now I have been
moving towards all my life. It is nearly here.

BOLD VIRGIN KNOWING

Quickening, innocence grasped.
She quickens and turns, trembles, harp strings played,
    delicately fingered
and her womb is no longer empty. What wisdom spreads
    through her mind,
limbs, bright joys and old fears, intimations of prayers and a
    nation's hopes?
Unborn child conceived without passion or sex yet
    intimacy, a being known,
knowing intercourse and communication.
Virgin, wild untouched still as forest primeval, undiscovered
    island, sea's
hidden volcano. What seed was dropped softly into your
    acquiescent heart?
As it lay trembling beneath words—covered with the wide
    hand of God.
Covered. Imprint impressed, swelling to ripeness of summer
    out of season.
Nature bypassed. This is mystery,
    so much humanness and yet so much lack—
only female form to make male flesh.
God's refuge in a girlchild's body that will learn grief as the
    only ground under his feet.
She rocks cradling herself and what's to come, singular
    witness for awhile.
Quickening, all eager desire, intent on her lot, her portion,
    her cup.
Over the roofs the swallows and larks drop, swooping and
    the vines climb
trailing fragrances in the night air. The wind barely stirs.
    Peace has slipped into the world.

Heat bouncing off the street, sweat running down my back
subway sweat wending way through crowds to shuttle to
    42nd St. E
A woman in what was once white clothes washed over years
Salvadoran—Guatemalan?
Alone with space around as she walked slowly in her world
Eyes cast down, lips moving. She was praying
As sure as any monk in a cloister, or sitting on a cushion.
Same chi, same sense of reverence in unself-conscious
                absorption of the Holy.
I was stunned—thrown into Your presence as she passed me
    by—
Oblivious of all yet somehow more solid in her communion
    with you
than any who hurried to their destinations.

I smiled and realized—she's already there, just being here.
When I am old may I pray and walk and be like that, O God
So simple, pure and true to myself and You.
Unabashedly Yours and about Your business, as my life
fades from cleansing like her clothes. Amen.

A DAY IN NEW YORK CITY,
BACK OF A SUBWAY CAR

Heading downtown express
           across the aisle, an elderly man talking aloud to
                  himself
loud enough for all to hear
about food—a specific hot dog
a place where it used to cost 45 cents
now $2.45! Same bun and dog, which he really loved.

Not far from him a burly black giant of a man
biker duds, chains, leather, hard face like his
thick steel-toed boots. He unrolled a wad of bills,
peeled off two single dollars
leaned over and gave it to the man—
In a surprisingly soft tone—"Here, old buddy, have one on
    me."
He took it. No words, only a nod.

One stop later, a lady got on, disheveled,
colors mismatching and singing at the top of her voice,
straw hat in hand begging—no one gave her anything,
didn't even look her in the eye—except the old man.
He took one of his two dollars and reached out
and gave her one.
Though she kept singing, silence lurched in all our guts
as the train raced on—
Lord! A parable dropped like a thud in all our hearts.
I found that I was crying soundlessly for joy
and for truth's sad tale told today.
I will not forget soon.

Lupita, Louisa, Ophelia, Henrietta, Rose, Priscilla, my
   widows, my women friends
all older than me by twenty, thirty, forty years and more,
   all having outlived, outlasted
their longtime lovers and friends. Solitary now, after long
   togethers. Separated, severed,
from promises that still hold their souls. We share much in
   common—me, their singular,
younger (by their standards) friend, who has never known
   anything but their newly stumbled
into dazed long loneliness. We understand each other, look
   knowingly beyond exterior things.
Virgin wildness can be known again after long fruitfulness
   or long emptiness in spite of biology
or theology's adamant assertions. There are some things
   the old, the widowed, and never taken and
kept know, like God who gave up divinity's wholeness
   for humanness and then let go of that again.
Virgin has more to do with passionate single-heartedness
   of soul than any experience of loss,
of handing over of oneself. Faithfulness begins, then
   becomes endurance, then lastly is born as
innocence restored. These are the first things one learns
   alone. We know. We know.

REVELATION

Christmas Eve Day. I turned over and over and then . . .
I woke to expectation: to emergences. I lay in the dark
having hid there for days cocooned against deprivations,
violences, miseries of the bloodiest of all centuries humans
    have inhabited,
not solstice, not even the blaze of moon so wide-eyed
closest to us in 133 years, no natural phenomena. No—
    unnatural
the unlikely event of divine intervention, becoming flesh—
The incarnation of peace, an atoning afterbirth, an umbilical
cord to home left behind as life-line, to be found
    everywhere, by everyone.
It was a given, as undeserving as the smeared colors of
    morning,
the pinks, the hues of blue, soft purple and silver glinting
    before
the sun's eye, stilling, hiding behind the hills.

Tonight is the night. This child of ages will be born.
Wonder-Counselor, Father Forever, Peace breathing quietly,
first-fed on a woman's awe and rocking arms. I will assent.
I do believe. All earth pushes and strains against the century
    past.
Child, be born in us tonight! Amen.
The world turns over and awakens . . .

VICARIOUS VISIT

The women's hands move over the bark, the spread
    paper/cloth
Pinpointing dabs of color, dots meticulously placed, their
    fingers dreaming,
Map-making, walking home. The route well-traversed.
Now it is there for those whose soul is aboriginal and
    knows where to enter,
and if to ever exit. For all others meaningless marks,
    eloquent or mute reminders
that there are so many other worlds than the one you or I
    live in. We must dream or die.

                      —for the women of Alice Springs, Australia

Blessing for a People

Indigenous subcultures, conjuring survival, water in desert,
    familiarity in unbroken expanses,
Security in wildness. Who are these marvelous people?
    How could we have treated them so
callously? Magical men and women walkers? Diviners
    treated more harshly than any
environment. Now their magic is to remember,
    to dig beneath concrete for the old markers
to know home. Coffin-trees, disperse grog-iness and claim
    their power once again.
I must trust and walk behind in awe at my lack of sense or
    perception and walk in their
united art of sound, sight, smell, their wisdom and my utter
    lack of understanding that makes
me dangerous. There are runes of track, chant, carcass,
    smell and shift of sand, veils in stone,
blood-droppings, scat. Follow. I dance. I disappear from
    here and find myself pass the veils. Rejoicing.

INCANTATIONS

Chants, psalms, plainsong, words caught in a choked throat, the unwordable, yearnings seeking a way into form: all the Spirit pulses and beats, rhythms of human heart and soul in concert, communion, and dislocation from the Mystery seek expression here. We live here. We live where we were conceived, birthed, raised, wander, settle, and gypsy, but always there are memories hidden deep within us—of the garden, Eden, heaven, the Kingdom of God—not so much a place, though it is that too, but a relationship—the one relationship that sourced us beyond lineage, genes, family, before birth itself. Zen folk call it our "original face"—earth, life, every detail and circumstance seems to be a mirror that reveals that reality back to us.

That reality—who we are with God—all of what we were once dreamed by Mystery's design and wild exuberance of creation. These pieces speak of the far-ranging moments, knowings, stammerings, and strainings after that mystery of belonging to the Holy and all else is really One, even here and now.

Here, prayer is often the word used to remember and to sink deep into the marrow of mystery, although these prayers can drift, lunge, and hang in the air as often as any are sent straight home to the heart of God.

These poems, too, remind us that prayer isn't something you do. It's also something that is done to you, as in "preyed upon." Or it is something you are—a praying human being most at home just being in the presence of Mystery.

God's strongest word is silence now.
God's poverty grows with distance from incarnation.
Flesh gave mystery some solidity that is long fading
like snow that seeps deep into earth.
Still here, but so diffused and altered radically.
This Lent was a labyrinth—What do I know of God?

It will flame.
Pentecost remembering draws near. So much heaped up,
dry leaves, withered branches, dead wood, old rags, lost
    dreams
ready for a spark, a flicker, of flame.
It will burn
it will come loudly shaking structures, around the corners,
over the roofs and it will seep through all the rooms with a
    rich
thick smell of burn, fragrant wood incense rising.
It will lick
speak in tongues hot passionate freedom, crossing over
    languages
conquering barriers of isolation until each head bears a
    crown of glory,
warmth, haloed softness, lovely by light.
It will flame
earth held in cupped hands, warmed, offered carefully
    tended, watched
protected, stirred into roaring crackling fires—of justice,
    and judgment.
Of hope and fierce courage against raging cold, melting it
    all with mercy.
It will come. It will be the last word, a tongue of desire,
    eager to kiss and to succor
This wind of fire. This hearth glow of God, come and dwell
    among us. Amen.

Silently seeking solitude, my hungry beggar's soul
then an alms is given unasked for—
a lone small bird walking the tiles of the roof.

Rain in my face, uncommon cold
whipping soft pink and even quieter white blossoms
off their branches, swirling about me, covering hair.
They could have been snow flurries,
except that the calendar insists mid-May.

Shawl wrapped tightly around shaking shoulders.
I stand until the stillness lies so deep—that I sense
underground the volcano is preparing to burst.
Spring unsettles, yet speaks so surely.
It's word—-be born!

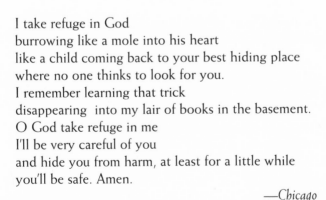

I take refuge in God
burrowing like a mole into his heart
like a child coming back to your best hiding place
where no one thinks to look for you.
I remember learning that trick
disappearing into my lair of books in the basement.
O God take refuge in me
I'll be very careful of you
and hide you from harm, at least for a little while
you'll be safe. Amen.

—*Chicago*

Whisky and water sunlight
the first drink of night
Each time is like the first time
I come as to communion
roll it around in my mouth
taking all the golden glow within.
Taken
the words of the toast are silent
All lifted up
sniffed and swallowed.
Who drinks who?

I want to be remembered for having wove the Word
subtly through every fabric and design, hiding it and then
uncovering detail, color, thread and line.
Wrapping all of earth and all its creatures in a cloth
fair, delicate and fine, that held a people's hopes and bread
and fragments and pieces of heart to raise the dead.
I want to be remembered for having shorn the sheep
and gathered wool, and spun and carded and made
    garments
against the cold. And then to have weathered all the storms
and dwelled in the high mountain passes and found the
    deep and
greenest grasses for their hungers. And stayed, keeping
    watch
over them, singing and humming them home, with the
    Word. Amen.

                            —after teaching in Ireland

Night rain running down the panes, wet memories and fresh
    places
in the darkness opening like entrances to caves. The
    sound—soft drums
aboriginal feet, following paths in my ears, straight into my
    stomach,
gently rubbing circles, song lines, weaving patterns of
    wholeness inside.
The rain bright boundless freeing building up into torrents
    of joy in my soul.
The wisdom of night dark waters murmuring in their
    wombs, heart beat
growing strong, yearning, pushing, pulsing, birthing a child
    that slides out
into mud and laughs aloud, alone with all its ancestors and
    old friends.
Animal joy, pure human gasp as I am cast out into the river
    downstream.
God is fly fishing in the rain and I am the line snaking out,
    thrown clear—
sent into the kingdom to catch another. am I dreaming,
    being dreamt?
Dream time, keeping watch at the window. I am awash with
    wildness once again.
No stars only the eyes of vanishing dew. My heart learning
    the beat
without the drum, swaying in silent places, suspended——

GAUDATE — RIBBONS OF JOYOUS LIGHT

So God-thirsty. So blessed. So tired physically.
Need for asceticism rises like a mountain thrust up by
   ancient heavens.
I sit and know what Advent really is—the coming of ecstasy
but pain beckons us forth. We are crouched in our crevices
     and our souls are hiding from the Holy. Each year—
the wrenching, each year we seek to do it with the grace
       of clouds hanging in the sky or water sitting
         serene,
or air utterly still as it was in the beginning, is now and will
   be
       forever—truth in words reaching for our flesh.
Come hold fast, O God, and sing your way home in us.
I awake to morning's first soft light and blessing and God
   coming.

Scriptures lie open on the floor
open door
the wind comes to leaf through them
stilled, I come to read the Wind's finger
pointing to my life.

In the shadow of Charing Cross I sit
Across from Galileo bent solidly over calculations—
>   Intent on measuring the universe. Intense
>   passion.
Inside—treasures of words, scribbles and scrawls of
    centuries.
The one I cherished seeing most—Gandhi's letter before
    gong on
>   A 21-day fast protesting the violence that
>   followed the salt demonstrations.
Eminently legible, untouchable under glass—the measure of
    a human being—
>   Meekness—gasping the vital essence of the
>   truth.
My back up against a wall warmed in the noonday sun
I reflect on my words—are they lasting? Or everlasting?
Ahimsa. I too vow and bless the Word made flesh
And cross that altered any measure of what is human in the
    universe.

—London

ENGLAND

Here sky and sea can get entangled, confused
no boundaries . . . Can be lonely—
or stunning, eliciting sheer terror. Drown in sky? Step
    lightly out to sea?
Crystal glint of shining escape grey clouds
Shadows thrown in daylight. Rain washes them away—
    where dreams go—
And then that golden light that tears away all semblance of
    solidity.
Waters above. Waters below. Waters welling up and
    overflowing.
The real Holy is made of tears, at least here.

❉

WHITE

White hot, gold bright, intense white, gold-white, silver,
linen, alabaster, ivory, shell sheen, island, sand blasted,
resurrection/easter white, beeswax, enamel, moon, sun
white, blinding, blasted, splendiferous, teeth, flesh, bone
white, cloud, polar bear, ermine, fox, lace, satin, natural silk,
cotton, wool, vestment white on white, threads
embroidered, snow, hail, fog, mist, air glorious pure air,
fresh after rain, cold bright white, parchment, feather, glass
sheen, water screen, meringue, wedding, funeral, death,
ashen, chalk, eye, rage, cold, fear, awe, pure, heat,
martyrdom, vanilla, cream, winter, clay, hope.

Poems are my practice (like waves are practice of water)*
like humming, drumming, moving my feet in place,
    chanting alone, praying.
My song this season is snow
flurrying, soft on the wind, wet, falling in sunlight,
icing on my hair, flowers in the bare trees, soft sound of
    mornings,
melting, dripping as it disappears, seeping into ground,
    freezing,
drifting against fences, crunching underfoot, pining in the
    moonlight,
satin at dawn, purity on my tongue, cold tear of losing and
    longing,
flaking, crystals invisible, white bed of sky, spirits, so many
    spirits
revealing themselves to us. It snows practically every day—
    I am slow,
need the repetitions. I listen, ears empty, eyes wide, skin
    drinking,
and the song slowly gives itself to me, rising and coming
    out of my voice.
All the words on paper are discipline, waiting for the song
    that has no
words just snow sounds singing me.

When I am gone back to ground, my song will stay
singing in the air, dancing in the snowfall.
And sometimes when I practice crow comes or raven
visits and they sing. They are the true singers.
I am honored that they come and carry my small song to
    Spirit.

* David Steindl-Rast's phrase

What did I do today? strange litany—prayed, lived with
   weakness, struggled:
didn't win but didn't lose. The list goes on—purified
   another, wrote poems, slept by day,
worked by night, destroyed schedules to reflect soul,
   seeking to grasp a toehold lost on earth.
Didn't do what was supposed to be done so that what was
   needed could be attended to.
Necessary incursions, incisions, massive revisions: chewed
   fingernails uncharacteristically
to bone. Was preyed upon, lived with sorrow's loss, missing
   another's sadness and then
took it away, gratefully, am still longing for home, yearning
   for otherness, waiting for love,
as though this page was still empty. Some prayers are not
   completed.
There is no Amen, just the invasion of divinity in such
   human fragility. And out of what
I was given, and not; I gave.

My real morning praise, I must admit, are not the psalms
      or organ songs in lighted monastery choir . . .
No! it's the deer darting, standing still and eyeing me softly.
They question my very presence . . .
Am I a threat? Am I a friend?
so full of motion, so full of grace, so quickly gone like God!

Days and nights reading poetry
pages scanned and studied
right to left, eyes hunkering back
to the original Irish (or Spanish)
along with the sturdy stone walls
of every road and country lane,
I look at them and begin stone by stone
to steadfastly dismantle them.
Marvel at the fittings in each space and then
try to reassemble, replace each piece where it had been.
Translation, reading the words aloud
tone, tripping forms, dense layers, lines
revealing hiding uncovering questioning.
Dance steps without music, left to right,
breathe, right to left, sliding open doors,
windows, continuums, going home, leaving,
adventuring, return backwards and forwards
in time, voyaging across channels, island hopping
learning the tides and currents dangers and deadly places
and stars to steer by.
It is the only way even if I do not possess the language
but have inherited the tongue. Read think bilingually
bi-ritually, bilocate, incarnate as the words become flesh
again.

The wind slams my door
And sneaks around the corner
My heart lurches free.

January bites my toes
clad only in socks
But, ah, the sun's kisses.

Light so strong I squint
Sky so blue it hurts
January's sun-drenched snow.

You are so close, God
Like snow on my tongue
And the sky above

Perched on a small porch
I sit, a bird in is nest
Warm and wrapped in wool.

Heaven starts right here
its back porch is this valley
and I just got home!

My afternoon nap
I fade and I melt
Wondering if this is wisdom.

Ragged lines—calligraphy?
Lovely—hard to read
even for natives.

I fall into sleep
Watching the snow melt.
Maybe I'll disappear too!

The moon tells me its stories
They seem so sad yet
Silence melts sorrow!

I am so hungry
But mind and stomach are full
Thank you very much.

My heart in my throat
tears just below the surface
Snow slides off the roof.

Eyes closed facing sun
serape wrapped around me
Snow and my soul melt.

Hungry, I eat words
Empty, I watch snow
Peaceful, aching communion.

PROTECTION RUNE

The protecting circle of the God of the Elements, of Gentle
Christ, of the Abiding Spirit, be keeping me (us) safe.

An old wish rises at night along with moon's eye
I awake and reach towards it as the whiteness fills the bed
It is ancient pure true. It is about communion, repairing the
world
restoring kindness and making whole. Radiance streaming
through
It swells. It is swallowed inch by dark inch. It sleeps. It
blooms.
It is always present, just hidden at times, waiting to stir and
enter again.
It is the one thing I obey ceaselessly.
Moon opens the tomb, the trapdoor, and I fall into
resurrections
as it falls upon the earth. It is as small as owl or my
eyelashes opening
and wren's body, but it looms a standing bear, a beluga
whale, a sequoia.
It is enduring. Am learning. I am apprenticed to
grandmother moon
and grandfather night. In rare darknesses it is rapture.

Snow always sits still.
Disappearing slow.
Nothingness nada all gone!
                I think I'll go the same way
                Oops. I catch myself
                And smile again.

———————※———————

Advent—ah—I ache for silence
as deep as dark as moon wanes
and the constellations shine.

I strain to hear the universe's cries
the star's singing and all mortals
whispering "yes"!
Come. We're waiting. Come.
It is anguished praise
but hope's finely tuned edge
is resonating steadily.

I sit intent. Advent Zen.

SEPTEMBER BLUES

porcelain vase against the cream wall
old bruises fading on fair skin
herons dusky in late afternoon heat
small flowers part white, part purple
fluttering against dry green leaves.
Eyes of a robin's egg though more lasting;
blurs of memories, faces long and newly dead
silk brushing and sliding liquid against skin
and a feather found in wet grass—a jay's discarded shirt.
Lilies letting go. The line between night and day
veils around the moon on an evening of thunderstorms.
Water in deep caverns leaning heavily towards the luster of
ebony.
Obsidian wings flashing in bright light while raven and
crow
bicker and clamor for attention.
Iris petals light on the fringes of violet.
Lavender and thistle, corn and bells wild in fields
and old veins rich in the arms of a widow
tears on a face allowed to fall
bones of a deer picked coyote-clean
fur on the paws of wolf in a trap
held in steel dull and deadly.
Just blues.

I want to write a hopeful poem
beak open the egg shells with gleaming whites and thick
        suns of courage
and make a cake of brownies rich and chewy.
I want my plants to flower now.
I want to take my finger and touch ever so gently the lined
        faces of friends
and honor the many wrinkles in the old, turning the creases
        into crinkles of laughter.
I want the hate, the rape, the fighting on huge and small
        scales to stop. And
I want peace to be taken up as international pastimes,
        obsessions and addiction.
I want earth and my hearth and community to feel like it's
        home, a dwelling place
secure where the poor can't wait to open the door after the
        long day.
I want hope to roll up her sleeves, stand and resist and cuss
        and sing
and catch everyone off guard. Make it be so.
I want this fall to be one of harvest and hope. Amen.

Early in the sunlight, the hawk criss-crossed my path
—home from hunting or out on a lark.
The familiar flap of wings slicing air
—effortless knife-like clarity given.
That wild-winged one has taken up residence in my mind.
It has become a day of vows to save 10,000 things
And a day to collect great aches and small sorrows
—left scattered everywhere.
What is sometimes termed compassion
—is also crucifixion.

Some take refuge in the Buddha, the Dharma and the
    Sangha.
I find refuge in the poor, the truth and the Trinity.
But I often splurge on stories (words), mystery and pure
    pieces of wildness
—given to me by The Holy Ones' pure kind magnanimity.
I then vow reciprocity—the least I can do for a lifetime
Bowing in sheer gratitude, along with late-night longing.

Chin in hand
Elbows on the sill
I watch the trees
Content with green
Some simplicities border on near-ecstasy.
And then, across the new cut grass
Comes a fox, gleaning in the moon's soft light
Moving with liquid ease, proclaiming
All that I survey as simply
Home to him.

                                    —Dublin

I ache for transcendence, being known by the Holy.
My body does not know its place. I go from shock, grief,
      fear, submission, hope, peace, to more—just
         wanting to go down another level into the walled
            canyons
of my soul. I am calm—restless calm, almost too aware
        of time near stopping and my own heart and flesh
not knowing what to do—heart ache, heart attack—
      incarnation's
        intimations of nearness and impassable separation.
Abruptly a reprieve—was it death I was approached by or
      the Holy?
Either way I was not ready, yet had to be. I am more so now.
Advent near Gaudate. I rejoice. I live still.

November's torn remnants
>   tiny solaces betray despair's shadows and I am intent
>   on restorations, miraculous healing

and simply repairs on the world and all those who dwell
    therein looking for a home.

I buy delicate cut flowers forced to bloom out of season,
    pale pinks of roses and canary

yellow mums as gifts—deceptively inserting beauty and
    smelling the hushed incense of loveliness

that defies isolation. I tell myself the mantra of plain thanks,
    gratitude when words do not go

where my heart is exiled.

In the litter I am a gleaner of glory. In the unmerciful
    insensitivity, I cry loudly with the crows.

In the death of the sparrow—it flew straight into my
    window—I stoke its velvet softness

decrying the end and take its winged spirit deep within.

The trees are filled with dead leaves that do not fall and I
    want to shake the tree and shake out

my head and burn it all, making smoke of sacrifice, needful,
    necessary, vital.

I will not bend to loss that is not part of the pattern but
    made of hate or rage or lack of love.

I will not. I vow, instead, kindness, attentiveness and tender
    regard, even if I feel like a bag lady

going through the garbage pitied and avoided by those
    who stumble upon me and see.

I will kiss, unsolicited, all and anything that stands or drifts
    into my presence. I claim grace.

I am determined to dowse and find water in wells of
    loneliness and underground springs in empty

spaces. I will brace myself against hate and meanness. I will
    move towards the unseen music.

I will linger with the poor and the outcast even with loss
    and stoke its edges.

I will beg leftovers of love. I will remember and put back
    together all the brokenhearted ones.

(continued)

I will savor anything of worth and be simple. I will be true
to you.
I will be human and divine and note all that serves life.
I will greedily collect scraps of laughter and trigger
avalanches of awe. I will burn. I will.
I will dance with the wind and court spirit. I will weave a
new time, a warp that holds.
I will be gentle. I will nurse those who hurt with a pelican's
intensity.
I will be an owl seeing in the dark and spider spinning webs
to catch the world.
I will search out what stuns and sparks and if necessary, I
will breathe underwater.
I will build a bridge, driving rivets into steel with skin and
fingers leaning hard into the work.
I will deny all that does not engender justice and heaven's
gaze.
I will not stop looking with both eyes at what kills, destroys,
so I will know its beginnings
and I will warn early and disarm and resist.
I will practice peace. I will lift up what falls and grows
unsure. I will hold you fast but freely.
I will uncover every trace of ordinary strength. I will lay
siege to God and subvert despair.
I will soothe with myrrh. I will regard you with forgiveness.
I will befriend God.
I will not forget hope. I will do what is right. I will wait on
wild possibility.
I will do ceremonies that make holy. I will touch you inside
and stop the pain.
I will be a child birthed out of time. I will dream and sing
the world a lullaby and kiss
it to sleep after screaming at the nightmares. I will seed
ecstasies in open fields and window pots.
I will your presence in our midst again. It is Advent.

The tall trees' branches blow side to side
like a mane of thick hair caught in a gust of wind.
It is eveningtide in an August drought.
We are all starved, crazed at any sign of rain.
A tart fresh small of it? A drop of moisture on skin,
A darking cloud, an aching muscle—all raw material
for anticipatory rejoicing and extended expectation.
Dance trees, shake, sway, freely submit
to the breath and guiding arm of the wind.
I am sister to your gyrations; my roots are thirsty too,
My limbs longing for a wet kiss, my tongue is stuck out,
head back, hoping for a taste. I pray aloud: Come Sky—
spit at us, cleanse our smudged faces and limp spirits.
Come water sprite—spit at us, let loose your torrents.
We will thank you with our tears of joy.
God it's like being teased relentlessly, a new way of
     water-torture.
It never did rain that night.

Ragged crows, dried leaves
Hot September makes us droop bent and slow
As the caw-cries echoes in our souls—
Summering, still but inevitably
we ripen, for the earth's eating.

Ah rain
Faint slanting lines, "soft" and so silent
      Yet always it evokes such sadness, tears on cheeks,
      wet to the touch, looking out through windows
      streaked and running.
All day it builds until it could be a din of voices, cries
      from within that will not be stopped—not misery,
      but hurt, ancient pain that drenches us.
Incantation, mesmerizing, trancing, piercing to bone and
    soul.
Then finally it purifies and sings in a fresh wash of freedom.
It is just rain, banishing all sorrow now—
just rain, reign of the just.
Lastly it is just a lullaby to ease the heart-sore
      and return us to sky and sea.

                                      —Dublin

I murmur *veni sancte spiritu, veni sancte, veni* . . . over and over
and over
A foreign language, one we only used to sing, to chant, to
praise together.
The words themselves a mystery, no meaning but the
cadence and the sound
Oft-repeated, even without knowing we sensed we were
pleading,
Standing on a threshold, but still in between here and the
veil that hovered everywhere-
Near.
A hand seemed to stroke the tops of our heads—soothing,
comforting, so singularly
and we were one for a few seconds. Amazing even as
second graders we could touch
the transcendent and only later know the word for it . . .
I think I could do without the words now—
and often long for the flow and the beckoning
that invited us so surely . . .

INTRUSIONS

Earth is such a wild, sprawling, splendiferous, and dangerous place to live. And there really are no borders or boundaries except the kind weather and geography and time draw on ground and in sky. And the world is so peopled—all those billions of folks. Yet that doesn't even begin to number the presences that Mystery has left here to intrude upon our habitual being or when we grow slack and unawares. There are grasses and herbs, trees "the tall standing ones," "all my relations" as the indigenous call them—the winged ones, four-legged, six- or more legged, creeping things, the fish, and those that waddle on land, soar the skies, and skim the waters—we inhabit this place with so many others.

They, too, have knowledge, reveal the Mystery, are a part of the hymns of the universe—languages of tracks, scents, leavings, hiddenness. Just because we do not take them into account or honor them does not mean they are not here or are not related to us, or that they are not our teachers, sharing food, space, even life and death, with us and because of us. Other than humans, there are creatures above and below and spirits galore who can summon us beyond, whose presence can be invading and intrusive. They can be sheer gift, Mystery's foreign, wild and other-worldly ways of getting our attention, playing with us, and reminding us that we are not alone and our place here is not necessarily meant to be the center of attention.

Usually I stumble when I intrude upon their worlds and when they intrude in mine. I always know that Mystery is very very near and clamoring for my attention, raw in its reaching out for me and its seeking a response. These poems are leftovers of such encounters, wonderings about how I and all of us react when Mystery intrudes in forms that we often are not at ease with.

Driving north to Santa Fe. An hour into sky . . .
Alongside the mountains are good company.
On the other the red mesa sits, a table spread
        though in this morning's light it is more an altar
        touched by the shimmering light of candles
        set for Mass. The elements gather.
All comes together in worship.
The air stills everything to an instant of serenity.
All is good, holy. I am, included, as much at home
        as chamisa or hawk, snake or particle of dust
        settled and lost in the sand. No sound
        but the one Spirit makes hovering.
All stops to turn. Maker approaches. We bow.
Caught and held. Enormous stillness.
Then I have to remind myself to breathe. Amen
                I carry mystery's scar.
                That note of the song is embedded in my skin.
                In stillness, night especially, I touch it gingerly.
                It aches, tingles—stirs, sings. I must take heed.
                It remembers one.

The animals beckon
the birds entreat
the fish lure
the insects pinch and nudge
they show themselves
revealing inviting,
their bodies pulling me into them.
Snake lies stretched out vulnerable at my feet-bare.\
Dragonfly dancing on my palm.
Dolphins' noses and songs in my dreams.
Doves nesting in my porch plants.
Jays chattering away at me, fussing.
Does and deer watching me draw near
their eyes wide, hearts heaving, but their hooves still.
The heron flies off with my heart.
The fish tickle my guts.
The wolf claims my nerves.
The wren makes off with my shoulder blades.
The swan and cygnet take my feet.
Why do they want me? clumsy, two-legged, slow, thick,
thinking too much, lonely, gasping for air, reaching,
    reaching.
Now it is they who reach out for me. How can I long refuse
such mystery, such frightening delight, so much muscle,
    bone, feather, scale,
eye, claw? Now I understand. The hunted gives itself
    fearlessly to the other
as gift, as final embrace. Both die. Both resurrect. Both.
I must go. Come to them soon. Their hunger taps mine.

Remembering amethyst light, blue lavender air, dark pines,
    pinon, cottony woods,
smoke sweet and hanging like ground fog. Serenity in
    between day and dark.
La Virgen de Guadalupe perched on a porch box with wild
    flowers, sunflowers, and Susans.
In the rafters above, olive sage drying out and cosmos high
    as my shoulders in the front field.
Then the trees along the horizon and mesa's line would be
    brushed black, then blur
into the rice papers of a rose-dark Japanese scroll, unwound
    slowly into night.
I sit. Hold my breath, thinking my heart would just stop
    from such stark delight
The birds would silently turn towards their home tree,
    crowding in thick as leaves.
And I would be washed in contentment, sitting in an old
    chair facing west,
just the virgin, mother earth and me, a lonesome daughter
    at her ease.
And the world would balance and come round right.

A blur of wings, a blur of hope
The ecstasy of red-winged black birds diving!
A bird hit the window hard, staggered
      but didn't hit the ground with its pyre of dead leaves.
Sun-spotted glass fooled it.
A piercing sound, but soft and low escapes
—I didn't know a bird could make that note.
Its rapture severed. Dazed.
         flying as though in seizure.
I grow dizzy just watching its route.
I partake of its erratic St. Vitus' dance.
I've known that moment that shatters pure joy.
Unself-conscious one moment and the next . . . .
        ordinary stumbling time reasserts itself.
        Sigh . . . . poor creature
I hope it recovers to fly again.
      It sits now on the stone wall
      and we stare at each other. My heart flutters.
Fly! I command it. Now. It does. And disappears.
Suddenly the world has come back into focus again.

Red Cedar Woman, your strength waters my eyes, burns my
throat and head and I dare not stand or walk in the north
wind. You are fierce and relentless in your onslaught. Can
we make peace, a pact? Smoke a truce, give gifts, come
together in a communion that does not reduce me to
avoiding you, huddling inside away from your presence?

I know the earth is torn, the air rent, the hill country
unbalanced, and that is why you hurt us so, you rant, you
attack. It is your agony you make us share. It has nowhere
else to go.

I will honor you, scatter corn, feed the birds and deer,
honor all the wild ones, tend to the earth, sing you songs,
leave you gifts, stroke each limb and lean against the sides
of your body. I will be kind and near and not forget you in
all seasons. Can we be friends, sisters, lovers, that don't
hurt? I'll remember your ache and understand and sleep
outside with you. I will blow you kisses, Red Cedar Woman,
and come and be familiar with you. I will bury my hair at
your feet and weave some graying threads into your dark
green. We will be braided together, as sisters do their hair
laughing. Please let us embrace and not hurt.

We can teach all the others and save some of earth. It
would, I think, honor the Great Mystery. I come to get used
to you and you to me, and be arm in arm with kindnesses.
May be both breathe deep and conspire together softly. I
cannot bear to miss the wind and hills and be without you.
It can be our secret. We will be thick as thieves, fast friends
who sing old songs together with delight. Restore me to
you, sister Cedar.

—after dying from cedar pollen allergies

SNAKES: PART I

    Second day outside Bangalore, stories of snakes
then that night a cobra got one of the dogs.
Ugly bloated, sickening.
From then on, every shadow, darkened place, movement
    unexpected
        I started, shook uncontrollably.
Calcutta more stories. Flooding. They floated in the waters.
More died from snake bite than drowning.
Pieces of me crawled all through India—when I walked
through fields waist high, or sidestepped dung, garbage
    piled all around me
        in what passed for streets and in bed in the dark—
    beseeching my ancestor
of the Emerald Isles for protection and posited belief in
    Scripture's promise
that we would remain unscathed—I still kept vigilant.

Illusions—as many as the snakes. Others all too real.
Sitting in June's garden, relaxing. Who should arrive but
    the snake finder—
Equivalent to water diviner.
Proceeding to walk the grounds, stick probing the surface
    here, marking,
here, there, markers—dozens of them—dig here. To find—
    snakes found
twisted, tangled, piles of them under every single spot
    marked.
My skin crawled.
Lord, I wouldn't want to have that kind of knowledge.

Delhi—Gandhi's grand avenue promenade, the long funeral
    procession
and snake charmers lining the boulevard. Cobra-hooded,
    rising.
My stomach turned over. One of them saw me, grinned
    sickly

(continued)

and headed straight towards me. I bolted. No way.
First day home. New Mexico. What did I see?
In my own backyard—snake. Not the deadly kind. Had to
 laugh.
Then I cried uncontrollably. Relief. Fear finally let loosed.

SNAKES: PART II

It is rumored that King David had trouble with
 spiders—
disdained them. When he sang his psalms and blessed the
 Holy One,
the Maker of All, he slighted arachnids. Later, in hiding
 from Saul,
it was the spiders who recognized him as God's anointed.
They spun their sticky webs all night and deflected
Saul's wrath and hatred—gave him breathing space.
He repented of his ignorance and disgust. Groan!

Litany: bull, rainbow, rattler, ring moccasin, water, strike,
 cobra,
garden variety, python, bless the Lord all you works of the
 Lord.
Slither, strike, curl, hiss, unhood, crawl, shed skin, sense our
 fear. Praise God.
Even as I flinch in my fear may I know the beginnings of a
 wisdom
That reminds me that there are depths in God I cannot
 begin to know.
Snake Maker, may all things serve you. And one day may
 the Child (and I) play by the
cobra's den, unafraid, as friends. Amen.

EL RECUERDO

(the gift/remembrance)

The porcupine was treed
in the dark it climbed
winding its way around to the top
scurrying roundly away from the long sticks
the water trails, the flashlights badgering it.
Finally a two-legged got crafty—animal crazy
and climbed the aspen tree clinging
precariously to cracking branches.
One thrust and the creature rolled to the ground
racing for the tall grasses.
But it was trapped
unceremoniously at long last
under a plastic trash barrel
marked and laden with three large stones.

There was a spoken understanding:
if the porcupine escaped overnight
it had earned its freedom
for sure it would remember to stay out
of the human's preciously guarded trees!

Early I came to check out the trap
he was long gone!
Reverently I knelt where he had been cowed
and collected all his spines
long white, silver and night-black points!
Relics of wildness to give as gift
to an Indian friend to sew into her moccasins and bag
they would bring his quickness, his love of freedom,
his binding but not limiting to her leggings and life.

(continued)

Later one of them brought me many quills
from the ten who did not escape the night hunters—
the cycle continues
life, death, life again.
Now I am part of the turning, the circling of the tree,
the wheel—
the porcupines have just moved south to New Mexico with
    me!

—Colorado

What is it about these images and objects that reach out
    towards me—
ledger-book stick drawings on torn-out pages,
Hankpapa shields and drums worn nearly through
brittle parfleche and deerskin shirts
petroglyphs, porcupine quills and eyes in stones and rock
    ciphers—
there is mystery, a sense of "once" still lingering, needing to
    be deciphered,
learned in old ways near lost. They are tracks, ways back,
    old languages
humming in my head. I know them. They know me. It's
    recognition,
painful, just-out-of-sight, beyond voice, in the wind, behind
    the eagles' wings,
under corn, on the edge of stars, melting in the sun's touch,
    long fingered, free.
The snake of time slithers around them all, saying: dignity,
    unutterable sorrow,
strength, waiting still to be seen, touchstones, arrows
    straight to my heart.
Slow like turtle I strain to understand and stand humbly
    before the old ones
still teaching, still trying to speak truth. Great Spirit,
    Manitou, give me eyes,
ears, senses to understand. My hands are empty. My heart
    is open. Come.
The sage and cedar burns. Even the pinon is for your
    presence. I will take
counsel with the winged ones: swallows, herons, hawks,
    jays, great buzzards
and honor earth and sky. And lastly I promise to care
    tenderly for all the two-leggeds
especially the children, the sick, the old and the poor,
    most beloved are your own people.
Inside this land indigenous hearts are strong. The drum
    sings. Listen. They are still here.

I miss my old magpies
in twos, threes and more. Their sassy squawking
their flash of black and white tail feathers
"twitching witches" I dubbed them long ago.
Their rude intrusions could always make me laugh—
even if a bit ruefully, as they robbed nests
and strutted on the fence posts, hard glassy eyes
always watching. They used to remind me of something
an Indian told me once: "those birds, they're like us—
survivors. It's our gift. Long after everyone else is gone,
we're gong to be here." I would rejoice to see even one
of those raucous angels come careening across my line of
    sight.
I'd take heart, grasp at raw nerves deep inside and hang on
for a dearer life. I miss my tribe these days.

COMPANIONS

A pair of night hawks fly overhead in formation trailing the
morning light behind.
Wren perches demurely on my railing, head cocked,
studying me, then decides,
lands on my arm resting on the chair and jumps to his
house—never showing
that he touched flesh instead of wood.
The cardinal arrives pushing all others aside, a crimson
streamer one would
expect a red carpet to precede.
Owl's mysterious presence lingers in bits and pieces, tatters
of down and baby
soft wing and the night's feast coughed up all matted like
beggar's hair.
The jay screams rude unlettered, tail in the air yet so true
to the eyes of sky
that one can't help but smile and admire.
Doves preen and puff, sitting on top of each other,
crowded all together on one small
piece of dead branch and softly sing belying their
awkwardness.
Sparrows, an army of them invade the cropped grass
foraging, cutting a swath
through birds, squirrels and seeds, hungry always, not even
dismayed by cat.
Buzzard circles, catches the first drafts of sunlight and just
soars high above.
I wait and watch, willing it to come close. It does and banks
eyeing me and turns

(continued)

to take the air upwards again. There are no outcroppings of
   rock to come in for a landing.
A tiny canary sings, darts fearlessly in and eats and sings
   and stumbles and sings and
retires to a branch just inches away and serenades me. I am
   elated.
These birds and I eat breakfast every morning together and
   hail my comings and goings.
I ask myself, when I travel on the road, do they miss me as
   much as I miss them—
and is it their cousins and relations that greet me as I
   journey? I think so.

A butterfly moved upon my face, and then another, three
    or four, more
pale white tiny thumbprint size, wings translucent almost
    blue.
The colors of a garden in Monet's Giverny, misty waters in
    the sky.
Rich resurrection flies tickling and fluttering around us
    whispering: hide,
cocoon thyself before you fly. This dying stuns all pain, not
    erasing memory
but gathering it into such light and air. Peel the membrane
    off of agony, go slowly.
It's a sure-fire way to get entangled with divinity.
    It is the glorious mark
of frailty stronger than great rocks blocking graves. Simple
    intricacies that
ensnare humans out to dump the garbage in the morning!
Blue wings, white wings—mid-summer morning's gift to
    heat-glazed dried-out
tired eyes that bring back daydreams of new-sprung spring.
I smile knowingly.
God spreads out night dreams across the sky of day
and then goes and names them angel wings, butterflies.
And he swarms sometimes around our faces.

Hawk swoops
Lands by a large abandoned nest
No sound but wings
Yet every creature knows!
Birds cry out
Chipmunks scurry and hide
It sits eyes hooded
Turns and rises
Gone.
The whole hillside
Throbs and pulses with vibrant life
Awareness heightened.
Fear, threat, presence evoked.
For me it was just awe
And sheer delight at wildness
Come to visit!

God are you out visiting
With eagles and jays?
Your tracks are still fresh.

Year of the tiger!
cub playing in grass
Soon it will be hungry!

Coyotes pre-empt the bell
Our timing in synch
we've been praying together.

Crows eat sun
flying home
Delicious sky.

Essence of bluebird
Not even a cloud
Mountains of snow I sit still.

Heart races, mind bolts
I watch as hawk hunts.
Am I hawk or the hunted?

Crow crouched
Night nibbling at
Tart persimmons. Autumn.

Chou-in Temple, Kyoto

Artful design, eminently practical, eighty feet of floorboards
  that when tread upon—sing like a nightingale!
  announcing intruders.
To those who know the subtle sleight difference in song
  between bird in the garden trees at night, sad
   and longing—
  and bird on the prowl bordering the monastery.
Silence, singing boards. I step lightly, stop, back track,
 step again.
It thrills a note or two at a time. It haunts—
  What part of my life signals intruders
  yet does not reveal that the heart has been sounded? Or
   truth told?
What nightingale's sorrow sings my longing beyond compare
  as I step unsuspecting upon my way?
If wood can sing at the touch of feet, what pray tell can I do?

The season is brown and bleak.
The ground thick dark as night.
Sky grey, lowering. The trees stand bare,
exposing old nests, thick lumps now top-
heavy in their limbs.
Grasses are thick with rust.
Fields fallow, clods overturned.
Earth seems to hurt.

Late November is so vulnerable
as it is stripped and goes to sleep.
I drive by at 75 mph and spot
a raptor alone on a bare branch!
Ah, it is a hawk day!
He's hunting dinner in the easy time—
No place for food to hid,
though food is getting scarce
in the biting cold.

Then suddenly it is dusk!
And the edge of earth bursts into flame,
dead ashes stirred by Pity.
The day's last moments
are bathed in burnt-out glory
. . . . peace settles subtly.
The Holy throws its cloak
over all that is cold and lonely.
We can sleep secure tonight
A hand holds us tenderly.

Slept in a borrowed bed
A friend's house at the side of an airport runway.
Deep thick, night full of dreams, full moon above.
A dream of snow, massive mountains; skiing downhill.
Wild abandon, body going down, leg broken.
The drone of an airplane taking off in the dark
Pulls me out of slumber to look at the moon.
>Sleep reclaims the night: a dream of a shepherd,
>   rough, careful
>One sheep, a lamb wandering away again and again . . .
>This time the shepherd moves, staff brought down
>   across
>His body diagonally, thrust out towards the lamb's legs.
>Its body goes down, leg broken.
>The shepherd gathers it into the crook of his arm.
>Shocked—at such deliberate intent, but I remember:
>Palestinian shepherds at the time of Jesus
>Would break the leg of a rogue lamb that strayed.
>The shepherd would carry it until the leg healed.
>By then it was so attached to the shepherd it would
>   never
>Wander off again. It dwelled in the shepherd's shadow.
>Another plane rises into the sky, its motor muffled in
>   clouds.
Awakened I looked out to see the moon,
Snowy white, full, hazy and indistinct but so full of tender
    regard,
Like the shepherd, in my dream.

—Good Shepherd Sunday, England

White roses scattered in a row
spied from a high window.
Late twilight bordering on the dark
(it takes is own good time here)
the cool finally enters stirring the curtains
bringing heart's ease.
Leaning on the sill, resting on arms
Posture reminiscent of prayer . . .
I really had gone looking for the moon
That last night at three a.m. had lured me out.
Cold shimmering, ice-white smoking softly
In the deep black sky.
Far too early for its rise, but I stay caught dreaming
By green disappearing, slurring, sighing its way through the
    shadows.
And white roses blooming blooming on distant bushes.
The luminescent memory—or a plain longing for bare
    shoulders
To shiver at the brush of pearls, a shower of petals, the
    smell
Of green dark seas, the wave after wave of gentle long skirts
Moving between legs—of a walk alone, long after midnight,
Of a woman still so young and then, the moon starts his
    climb.

—*Dublin*

Pyramid Lake
serenely blue-green
deceptively dangerous
an endless turquoise stone
at Indian head
we mired the old car in sand
and waited for a Paiute to come drag us free
His eyes smiled, downright laughed
we enjoyed being held by the ground too
that bonded us and we bowed to each other
caught on his land.
Then a furious run to the water
dragged down by sand so hot
it burned through the soles of the dog's paws
poor Louie and Caitlin, whimpering and dancing
in pain, jumping up on us, digging furiously
down looking for cooler ground.
We were ready to hoist them up on shoulders
90 lb weights, and lug them to the water.
Once there—all forgotten—heaven in salt water
shared only with cormorants and sea birds.
We waded, walked the edge, splashed, played
and watered, knowing we had to climb the dunes
again. This time, we filled water bottles, the
sack and anything to ease the fires of the feet.
Limping, frantic steps, running fast—anything
to stop the burning through. Exhausted, both dogs
dozed and slept the ride back home.
Our adventure, complete with a car as jittery
as any hurting four-legged. We laughed a lot
and enjoyed every minute of the jaunt, sun-baked,
wind dried, sand fried, water doused, rescued
by a stranger happy to share his ties to the land
with us—if even only inadvertently. The land
held us, locked us in embrace, reminding us who
belongs to who. Grand outing inbound.
Gracias.

Susans, the queen's lace, cat tails
fireweed, the flowers of high summer
I stand in corn, tasseling out below my knees
whatever grows in this year's season survives on
bare necessity and endures ascetically.
Overhead a black bird flies a small creature
dangling in its beak chased by a ragged line
of squawking crows.
The sky is layered in northern blues
thundering and spitting its disdain for the land's plight
cruelly teasing earth with precious sips
even that small dollop of water coaxes the smells forth
luridly accosting senses that are in the throes of long
    deprivation.
The psalmist's words
"Fresh and green are the pastures where he gives me repose"
    mock me
promise me, make me mourn for the dry weary places
    without water
mirrored in my own parched soul.

Ozone depletion.
the lake lies smothered under a thick quilt of smog
all colors of the spectrum seem artificial, eerie
strange beauty that is deadly. Darkening waters
grey sickly green air, the grass brown and roasted.
Eyes hurt, lungs ache, muscles stiffen
throats constrict, hearts skip, bodies resist
knowing they are being assaulted.
Mother the Earth, Father the Sky,
are you trying through your blatant pain
to warn us of our disintegration?
Are you screaming in rage against being violated so?
Are you pleading with us to be kind?
I hear you. I too silently scream, in a chorus of keening.
On the windowpane caterpillars spin cocoons
split that thin veil too soon and die forever, aborted.
interference has set chaos in motion. What are we making
in our torn atmospheres?

Vigilant nights and days, strung like fragile berries on dried
    out cut branches, falling discarded everywhere.
Reeking of grief, great battles and silent
    screaming before approaching doorways.
Solstice of winter, year's end. Soul shedding its covering
    vulnerable as any common snake.
Lines writhe across walls, stoles hung, draped on shoulders,
    borders broken, trespassed territories,
opening up, the unknown beckoning, drawing closer,
    becoming intimate, unbidden, rude even.
Body strains at places soul ventures, not heedless
    of danger but not cowardly either.
Resolute, set, determined—necessary vigilance.
    The winter watch—who is to say it is not the real reason,
the season turns, the year turns over, the light returns?
    The Triumphant inches daily,
unnoticed except by the vigilant. In the cracks comes glory,
    angel voices, starlight, the child
the doorway is open, the invitation is given.

Found: a snail's shell, a house left behind, brittle as an egg
    and as fine.
The color of parchment, the feel of paper along nails, tiny
    holes, imperfections,
delicate details, light as a feather. It gleams dully, this bone
    of snail,
the same color as its gleaming trail. It fits into the palm of
    my hand, snug.
I am careful, leaving it on a rock ledge in the cemetery
    among its elders
and pray—may I leave behind such a home when I depart—
    near perfect,
a finger's breath of beauty for an unsuspecting stranger to
    find and know
a moment's delight, a stab of reverence and awe and an
    entrance into eternity
through a spiral staircase.

                                                        —*Wales*

All the voices of the waters taking turns beneath my
    window. I vigil diligently
and seek to learn their names—notes, keys cadences, tones
    and how the wind
plays with them (through them) all. I listen intently and
    they come, repeating,
repeating, teaching me to follow, imitate and pick up their
    refrains. Mantras
washing, stroking, murmuring. And I wonder if what I listen
    so hard for—
and think I hear in the water's meeting the shore is silence
    underneath it all
or just God hiding below the surface of all things? I have
    to listen. It is a strain
that courses through every detail, each moment, each
    singular sound. Does it
hear me too? I wonder.

Night has entered in and filled every corner of sky. It
    happened quickly while
I read by the window. I looked up and the dark had opened
    wide its arms
and pulled everything close to its breast. Now I sit alone in
    the dark looking
out into the night's full presence and opened eyes. Very
    much at ease, at home
content and sad. Time keeps ebbing away. The tide turns
    and the water recedes
again. The night reigns for now. My eyelids want to close,
    drift towards that
intimate darkness. I succumb, easily seduced and held so
    completely and securely.
I turn over to sleep trusting that when I awake night's sister
    will be slipping into bed
with me, making room for herself and pushing me out to
    play with day. I always
soften under the voices and echoes of this place.

OUT OF THE BLUE

Blue dark of morning
    In occluded light from fading stars
    the trees are dimly sketched out.
Earth is becoming visible—slowly.
A lone leaf brushes my cheek
    as the wind blows it down to its resting place.
    Rough-cut silky touch.
It does not startle me—just passes by so near.
Earth in its immensity can still be so kind
    even without intent.
The least gesture and I am utterly undone.
Dissolving to that pinpoint just before tears
    and then the bells peal out
Summons to morning praise.
Out of the blue . . .

Dusk approaches dim and dappled, softening all the edges
of the day.
The air hushes except for the birds' twilight songs, sounding
more and more
like solemn benedictions and murmurs of mothers to their
babes in arms.
When the dark comes all is deep and peace haunts all the
corners of this domain
and solitude attends all those awake and dreaming.

A stand of birch trees on my morning path through the dark.
The bark peels, scrolls being unrolled.
What words, what messages are being passed on
                in this fall stripping down, exposing?
I peel and gather and peer at language
                I do not know but am fascinated with.
I trace my finger tips along the torn papyrus . . .
                reverently in awe.
Prayer—standing on my way—to monastery morning prayer.
I am witnessed, humbled, confronted and seen-through.
Strips of prayer now lie crumpled all around my feet.
I do not dare to take them home with me.
                They remain remnants on the ground
and in my soul.

The doe comes so close
before she sees me.
neither of us breathes—

Time stops while we look
each waiting for the other
To bolt or to breathe.

I'm the one who can't hang on
and I have to inhale
What was left behind?

Vividly her eye held me
Imparting wisdom
What did I give her?

An aureole of iris, lavender blues, purples, a rare black one.
The eye hungers from a distance, gazing on another's
garden.
Seeks to smell tho they are notoriously without that
enticement.
Petals hang, tongues soaked with dew. They stand straight
so dear, so distant so like April's aloofness, so alluring.
Night rains come harsh and with morning they are gone
And I am left bereft and forlorn, and so alone.

I stumble upon Spirit's trace . . . a sidewinder's trail, spied in
    sand,
        fills me with awe and down-right fear. I wonder how
            recent
        that track is and what that sentence says . . .
It is a language unknown to me—snaketalk tho I've heard it
    spoken
        a number of times before, always when I was alone,
            isolated
        and hungry for sun's blessing and the ways of going
            apart
and silence, like sand, makes the tongue clearer, the sound
    more intimate.
I crouch close, reading like one with poor eyesight,
        thinking nearness will aid in my interpretation.
The pattern captures me and drags me in.
Such calligraphy, such warning, such sheer exquisite
    dancing language.
For one leaping second I sense what it means and it sings
    its way through me,
sending me deep down inside, to that place where only I
    stand, or crouch
        before the Great Spirit's glance—sideways usually but
            for this instance
        straight on, wrapping itself around my heart.
The Holy is a sidewinder!

Old cypress trees along the Guadalupe River
great exposed roots, gaping holes in trunks
from violence; water, lightning, age, decay, flooding.
My friend goes to sit in one, scrunched and hunched
inside, comfortable in the wooded womb.
I too find a niche and snuggle down and in
and sigh and sit still back up against the trunk.
The tree wraps me round, embracing. We both
do a lot of sighing-breathing together,
limbs rubbing easily against each other.
Until I see a fat long snake just at my feet.

My heart pounds and I breathe in fast.
I'm trapped in this tree with that snake
not a foot away. We eye each other—from
rock and tree. It moves so slowly unwinding
stretching out towards me. I barely breathe
and push myself up against the bark harder
and harder. Nowhere to go.

I wait on a snake. Learn to breathe very
quietly. Learn every marking on that tree,
let alone every mark on that creature.
It was beautiful. Its lines so sinuous,
simple, intricate patterned, mirroring the
lines of cypress bark deep rich browns greys
blacks hues of plum purple lavender.
I begin to wonder: would the skin feel the same
smooth, life pulsing from inside, underneath
(like a tree)? Would he find my skin like his/hers
or like the wood, or rock?

(continued)

Abruptly he slipped into the water.
Gone in an instant—with my
questions and wonderings. I leaned back
into the tree, eyes closed contemplating
Texas trees, Texas snakes, Texas sky, Texas river
and rocks, fear gone, reverence building up,
gratitude becoming a weathered line in my soul—
learned from a tree and a stranger made friend, my snake.

I start thinking: do all hearts
feel the same, smooth, pulsing from inside
underneath, underground heart beating pounding
where we are all bound to earth? I sent out
an SOS message in my fear and so many responded—
touching me—my skin is still talking about it
and inside me is now a small place for someone
to climb into and rest awhile, ease down and sigh.

Now I know too that I love the snake in me that presents
itself—just resting on rocks and terrorizing folks.
I will stay there and hope that a few begin to see the marks
of the Maker sketched along my spine and face and tongue.
The snake is the balance to the womb's safety. It is the
lonely dangerous presence of Creator's imagination and
        nearness
and I love that stillness as much as the cypress wood's
        solitude
and quiet friendship.

I go back doubly blessed, the stone
lifted from my heart, my walls buckled and collapsing.
A day in a tree, attended to and visited by a snake—exactly
what I needed to be human again, and humbled and
        disturbed and reminded
that the snake that is wrapped around the wood heals the
        heart.

THE MORNING
OF THE MAGPIE

I left
the window wide open, curtains drawn back.
The moon is full and I wanted to be awakened
        by its intruding intimacy as it rose,
but I slept through the night
        and I was awakened—rudely by a magpie
        sitting (if it was ever for a moment still)
on the window sill inside the window frame.
The room is small
his presence
strong.
I lay in bed, bundled, one foot exposed
It hopped to the bed covers!
I was wide awake.
Two feet from my face
It hopped from foot to foot
It couldn't get ahold of solid ground
but sank into the duvet.

Lord, I thought—how will I get it to the window ledge
        again?
He didn't seem in any hurry to depart.
I caught the clock's face out of the corner of my eye—
        4:30 a.m.
The black and white and fierce blue wings rose up   V
I expected the loud raucous cry
        but silence filled the room.
I daren't move—but I wiggled my toes
(the ones underneath—safe from that beak!)
and feared for my other foot!

(continued)

Then I wanted to laugh—it was all so ludicrous
I was grinning deliciously, giggling like a girl—
Awakening in the morning to find myself in bed
        with a large clumsy magpie.
He must have suspected and became insulted—
(magpies do have that aristocratic air about them)
he turned his back on me,
looking for flight and hopped to the edge of the bed.
Then deliberately he landed directly on my foot
And used it for his jumping-off point—
It looked as though he grazed the window frame but he was
    free—
And I was alone in the bed again.

Trickster—I remembered—
I felt—investigated, probed, visited accidentally, curiously,
    honestly.
Disappointed that I might have rebuffed him by my
    unseeming
        lack of seriousness—
Perhaps his dignity had been piqued?
I slipped from bed and was enchanted—
to find he'd left a feather!
The avian version of Cinderella's slipper!
It is black—blue black.
Delicate soft fierce bit of night wing
I love its silken feel.
I call this day June 30, the morning of the magpie.

                                                    —Dublin

Late afternoon I head out to work out
and near drive right off the road
through the fence and into the sheep.
Towering above, straight in front of me
is a perfect gleaming double arch rainbow
shimmering translucent wild clear colors
falling over each other. I get out and stand
to face the vision knowing in my head
it won't last long, being made only
of moisture and light on the angle of where I stand.
The shades of hummingbirds, butterflies, iridescent
fish—greens, emeralds, blues, teals, aquamarines,
royals and all the deeps of waters above and waters
below, skimming, darting seas of roses, reds, purples
canaries, yellows and greengreys. It moves.
A blanket being shook out, a river snaking up and
down, rippling and then it's gone. I blink,
waters in my eyes. No wonder the Indians say
rainbows are made of birds and butterflies hover-
ing, shadowing, wings gently brushing past
and then, gone. The covenant is still honored.
The breath of the Creator still moves up and
down the stairs of sky coming and going. I pledge
to return the favor that bowed over my life
this day—until forever.

Frost and snow rinsed all the street overnight.
The canal still runs with icy clarity—a cold mirror
That reveals too much if you're not ready for such
   brightness.
Pines go blacker, camellias blush deeper, ice icicles glint and
   gleam jasper.
Earth turns white jade, fine porcelain, celadon—though it is
   only morning,
winter and a storm of flurries that cast such hues and
   textures and dazzle the eye.
I stand listening, watching, awed at such artistry, dazed at
   transformations.
Windchimes so serene I can see the notes, taste the
   after-silence.
These are inescapable entrances to caverns of light.
I'm rinsed clear—I stand in snow head bowed.
All is immaculate in this moment.

                              —*Kyoto, Japan*

Singapore Dusk

Silk, the cling of a long skirt as a woman friend walks by,
 blood spattered pavement
where a fish was dropped, interlaced with shining scales,
 the dart of a loose cat.
Vermillion dab on a forehead passing me, the scentless
 presence of orchids,
The smell of sweat on skin as rain approaches. The sickly
 hue of sky smeared
with pollution from across the Maylaysia Straits. A
 momentary hush. Even birds silent.
The city sighs—does it remember what it was before? The
 mangrove swamps,
tall swaying grasses, fishing and farming villages, dirt
 footpaths, an island in a sea of green
glory? And then the night barges in fast, obliterating
 everything. Just dark, heat, insects.

Past midnight there's a slight trembling in the air
The trees sense it first and brush against the glass
It reminds me of women rocking themselves in sorrow,
holding onto themselves lest they too begin to unravel in
     grief and loss.
It has an almost inaudible high keening to it and strangely
it is oddly comforting in its ultimate universality.
It only visits briefly—a couple of hours—thank God!
But it will not be lightly brushed off or easily forgotten.
It feeds a seed buried so so deep in each of us.
It whispers—mortality and vulnerability, kindly
but inescapable, the way truth is told to us
by One who knows and who loves us achingly.
One can only stand silent, trembling, known.
There is no other recourse.

Sky empty except for moon in early morning. Pale blue
     jade—heaven above.
Air fine spun silk threads tie me to eternity.
Silence seeping through me as snow melts into hard ground.
Cascades of joy splinter in bird song. Trees crack in the
     cold.
I stand feet going numb. Eyes water in the wind.
Tears are everywhere—all embracing purity, pain and
     pleasure.
Gentle justice sheen of spirit shining through heart-aches.
Stretch to hold it all however short-lived.
Pierced to the bone. Joy. Lustrous pearl without price.
                                        —*Kyoto, Japan*

SEASON'S FINALE

Mountain peaks bare boned
Clay colored jutting out above green ridges.
Trees marching upwards, thousands of
    toothpicks
Stacked against clouds tumbling over the front
    range.
White puffs, cream-colored ones and more ominous thick
  lumps
Stuffed with grey waters looking for the right place and
  moment
       To burst bonds. Still green, green—so much
       rain
Seasons of spring off course, lost in September.
  Wind soft but it has a cool hand as it caresses bare skin.
I laze wondering when this will come again.
      Just now, here, I steal some heat left over from
      July,
swat June flies and sweat like August.
      The bugs clack and whir; every creature
      knows:
This is it even as the storm builds up across the valley.
These last licks are the sweetest for being so short,
  coming at the end,
      slipping in one last time before bowing out.

INFUSIONS

Blood transfusions, vitamin B shots, vitamin C chewables, heart and organ transplants—unbelievable surges of energy, vitality, medicine for healing and strengthening. The spirit and soul realm has its ways, too—the touch of another coming unexpectedly, a stranger's intimacy, the poor's hospitality, a gentle stroking laid on violence's destruction, tears welling up over a slight detail—these are infusions of hope, peace, passion, freedom, plain graces and love.

The Spirit is the sacrament of the world and is always seeking flesh to use, to touch, to express itself. The Spirit is always seeking us—like a heat-seeking missile seeking its target; an arrow its prey; the eye of an owl for movement and carelessness on the edge of dark.

Infusions that bring soul medicine or bruising realities to bear on long ignored muscles of the mind and heart are in these poems—a story spun out by a spider web of circumstances, laughter erupting, hot lava of anger spilling loose—righteous prophet anger focused on souls too content. Electrical shocks, chi activated, disciplines of graceful motion that loose what is blocked and held bound—these instances are felt as though Spirit touched flesh, flesh touched back, or home was found in a foreign land as familiar as any well-loved place. Mystery goes out in search of friends, accosting and curling up around the unsuspecting. Poems inevitably are spit out, given birth to, wrenched out of such daring games of catch-as-catch can between Mystery and ordinary mortality.

A blue moon. Cold aura. Biting wind.
Skin feels like it should have teeth marks.
I walk—to keep warm—to be alone.
Sleeping in another borrowed house and bed.
A guest in another's space, but not treated as one.
More interloper, awkward presence, foreign body.
I will go back in, though my soul will stay outside,
more at ease, at home out here.
I wander with a Buddha-moon as company.

—Ohio

Martyred trees, flaring wounds, crowned in sunset's dying
     light.
It is brightness subdued and glorified.
Even a fractured fall is full of favor,
always tinged with fire and freedom's touch.

Mornings the lake water has a matte-finish
fog mists throw a mantle lightly over its wetness
softening, inviting, masking its underlying cold.
I sit and observe one still-life in slow motion,
same shutter, same spot, but ah, the light! the light!
          and time's passing . . .

Morning light startles
revealing what night held in its closed hand.
Vesper light comforts
concealing . . . and the hand closes over it all again.
Somehow shadows speak in such silences
and I listen, loving this dark's touch, so intimate
so intent, so true, so like You.

❋

Everything
       This day screams
Are you aware of how much love
             is loose in the universe—
Spin-offs, smells, perfumes, essences
Left behind when God glances or passes by?
Are you?

Buddha, red rosy cheeked apples, an offering to Kamakura
    bronze, weathered green.
Later monks will feast sinking teeth into ripe fruit.
    Mouth waters wondering at the thought.
Even greedy to steal one—Buddha would understand.
    Others hardly!
I so love that great Daibutsu creature. So full of peace,
    serenity, overshadowing all who come
        and looking upon them with such obvious
            affection and blessing.
        Always I hate to leave, backing away watching and
            only reluctantly turn away to go home.
        Mata—until—goodbye. I take you with me or you
            keep me here,
        Sitting between your perfectly positioned thumbs.
        Ah, such a place to rest.

—*Kamakura, Japan*

Along the riverbed, near dried out now, the grasses rustle
    softly whispering in the hot winds.
They weave and bend saying: harvest me.
    Make me into a basket—
It's easy. Just follow my lead and twist the plaits in the
    direction of the breezes.
They form before my eyes—is it memory or vision?
    When I leave
something has been rewoven in me.

THE VESPER HOURS

Ubiquitous
Omnivorous absence slips in again
A daily visitor here around dusk. I look forward to its
    approach.
It reminds me with blunt force that we are only residents
    here,
                Asylum seekers intent on a resting place if
                  only temporarily.
You know what it's like, you who "pitched your tent to
    dwell among us," stranger.
How imperiled we all are. Distressful certainty . . .
    it whispers impermanence and comes
    Hand in hand with its companion on the journey: fear.
Nothing is withheld. There is urgency—as starlight goes—
    for with it goes the gesture—
the gratuitous grace's intensity.
Dusk grasps a piece of me. Its hold is tight, a grip of reality,
But it is—so to speak—short lived.
Dusk is threshold—did someone say that? I step out
And stand in the doorway. Just here. Poised!
I retreat as day departs. Even if I'm often feeling orphaned
    and distressed
                I must equally confess, emphatically—that
                  I'm the recipient
                Of gladness, goodness, gratitude—I'm at a
                loss for words.
Each evening an epiphany and I go God-haunted to bed.
A sliver of mercy lodged firmly in my heart.
Night firmly closes the door again.
I lean up against it and know it is always left unlocked.
                —*Holy Ground, all holy nights, All Hallows, Dublin*

I read once a novel about a woman who lived inside a wall, an anchorite freely walled in, walled up in a small tomb, cave, grave. Inside she lived, prayed, impassioned dying life. Another brought her food, words, news of visitors, the outside, sunlight, commerce, and horrors. She had her own, I'm sure—it was crowded in there. Others considered her mad, demented, despairing, wise, holy, closer to eternity, divinity, than most cared to come while still here on hard ground. I remember being fascinated, awed, troubled deeply by even the thought, let alone reality. Now, however, I know you don't have to build the wall. Just turning towards and into pain will initiate you into that strange walled dwelling. The spirit's domain can be as demanding as any anchorite's freely chosen cell.

———————❋———————

A mile-long field of sunflowers ripe and golden
in late afternoon glow, ready for the picking.
Seeds, days end, just passing by, looking back
at all that bounty. Waiting.
My life is one long such field of hope.
Sunrise still to come.
I have so many promises with light
—a mile-long field's worth—at least.
Even with eyes closed and lashed for sleep, the sun spots
remain, tell tale signs of vibrant orange-yellow orbs, circles
    of my life—
of all our lives.

A glimpse passing by at 60 mph . . . poppies so orange red
and wild along the road.
Back at the house, someone has again planted giant peonies
all around the fire hydrants!
The buds are tightly wound shut soon to burst free. I walk
past them slowly each time.
These I will savor every inch and second and commit them
to memory, in case
I ever need such incomprehensible red for warmth.
Some things demand to be studied as survival techniques—
the making of lifelines,
the braiding of friends—the sweetness of solitude, the ritual
of an afternoon cup of tea,
—the vitality of secrets kept inside, the raw makings of a
story,
the decay of an ancient, familiar and leaned often against tree,
the demand of justice edged with mercy,
the scent of the poor that reek of God,
the catching of a glimpse of mystery out of the corner of
your eye—at 60 mph one day.

Crescent moon in the forehead of the sky,
the stars come out dancing, whirling, spinning in the dark,
sequined, silent. Impulse, shaking, a star trailing scarf.
The ground has gone russet in the shadows of dusk,
    burning fires in the smoke of sky.
I know now from experience that this kind of heat left over
    from day and the temperature
of night will lure morning fog into every corner and crack
    and lie thick above as though
land becomes sea.

---*---

I miss trysts with the stars. Here night invades but city
    lights and thick cloud
inversions block the sight of the small shining creatures of
    dark—the eyes of the other side
of the world. I miss the sense of being watched, held, and
    looked over from above
by distant spirits who, the Cherokee say, walk among us by
    day. They conceal
themselves in the light and are meant to dazzle and reveal
    themselves in the dark.
It has been too long a time away from star eyes.

Rain days. Water coursing down stone, shining alchemy—
    grey turned silver.
Sheep wet thick and clumsy in sodden fields, laughable,
    forlorn-funny, sad, all lost.
Black birds large against slick green glass of ground.
    Later as the day fades
to cobalt air in a shimmering embrace, spreading, gathering
    towards the night's quiet,
I stand all alone in a parking lot, scarf wrapped, hands
    buried in pockets, hunched against the cold,
the sky's tears running down my face.
    After a long while,
each single drop alights as a prayer—mercy's freedom,
    mercy's freedom, mercy's freedom,
free, come, become one. Mercy becomes a waterfall
    coursing down me.
Only the wind keeps me from turning into a stone holy
    statue—Instead, I turned
and tore myself loose. I turned the door handle and entered
    the house. I crept
into a borrowed bed—the quiet coverlet spreading over and
    under me wrapping me
in swaddling clothes to sleep, soaked, sodden with shining
    chrism, mercy streaked and smeared.
(First lesson in prayer—Rain taught me.)

                                        —*Glasgow, Scotland*

Night brings secrets, not obscure knowledge
        but luminous knowing.
It is kind with nakedness that is so clumsy
        and self-conscious in the light.
Bare reality demands and one can stand before it
                in the dark.
I have found a shortcut to the truth . . .
through the dark.

Fireflies gleam and glance
flutter in their dance
above wet grass.
Stars sprinkle and blink
pinpoints in a dark sea
above earth's mass.
Angel's visitations
gypsy's fire and ice
spirit's soft breath
on a summer's night.
I fall asleep on a bed of weeds
wildflowers fill my head
and the tendrils of wraiths
encircle my soul.
I am lost in a passing breeze
that sighs its way to eternity.
Content to disassemble in night's song
I rest somewhere in between the notes
A mote in God's great eye.

                            —*Chicago*

PORCH-SITTING

There is a ritual to this porch sitting.
First, if possible face the western sun, sit in a chair that's
    not too cozy
so you stay alert—put your feet up so you're off the ground
but close enough that you can reach down and touch it
    with fingers
stretched.

Bring water, not icy but cold enough.
Listen. Pay attention!, ears up, pulled back.
Don't miss anything, get distracted!
(I'm sure I could teach graduate level courses in this—-)
Sweat
feel it run in a trickle down your neck. Soak your shirt.
Don't forget to breathe. Really breathe!
Take it all in. Let it all out. Marvel at it.
The simplicity, constant repetition.
Be grateful. You are alive!

Drift. Pray.
Keep in mind that once you do this—-
—-commit yourself—-
you're going to have trouble coming back in.
Settle. Root yourself.
Feel it go down your spine and into your buttocks.
Stretch!
Make yourself longer.
Resist too much thinking.
A little is OK especially if it leads to dreaming
or a few lines of poetry or humming (you'll attract
bees, butterflies, hummingbirds and Lord knows what else!)

(continued)

Sometimes you have to do this alone, especially in the
    beginning
until you get the knack of it—
later you can bring another along but you have to be quiet
—-not just not talk. Be still.
Be stilled!
Try being a tree. Practice the seasons.
Smell—send out your senses, like tentacles, widening your
    range...
go octopus in a circle tentatively absorbing more and more
Lean into osmosis and then reverse the process
Disappear into this space.
Slide between the veils.
now, you're beginning to know the basics of the ritual.
That's enough for the first lesson.

Now you're on your own
Good luck with resuming your normal life—-
Laugh!
at yourself and dissolve all violence.
In returning hold the world very very carefully...
Go about making peace.
If you find the edge creeping back in—
Quick! Head for the porch—
Anybody's!
And start again. As tho it were the first time.
like when God first sat on the porch and sighed
and said: oh, this is good, so very very good.

Summer green pours down the mountain sides
Lush velvet sheens shimmering in heat's haze, bordering on
    blues
Insects, all manner of winged things buzzing, whirring,
Alighting on skin, getting tangled in hair, ants, bees, yellow
jackets, gnats add soft symphony to the louder sounds of
    birds.
They are all echoes against the background of stillness,
    utter calm,
Empty sound. Empty mind. Empty universe
Empty loveliness, to behold, to experience. To enlighten.
There is just this, all this, nothing but this, now. Nothing
    but . . .
This one note is pure
Even I, just here, doing nothing
Am nothing, but lovely to behold
Pure being true. Ah.

—*at the monastery*

I remember so often the long line of women.
    Indian pueblo people shuffling along the ground,
raising the dust, barely lifting their moccasined feet.
    Faces stoic self-contained, serene
hiding the real truth from outsiders
    laughing inside as they tickled mother earth.
They know she loves the feel
    of her children's feet on her belly.

Saturated sunlight.
I stare at one spot of lake water
　　　　　Breathing, concentrating.
The radiant sun kisses my skin.
I sit perfectly suspended—
　　　　　Not on the ground
Of rustling dull brown fallen leaves.
The smell of the wind is exquisitely sensual.
Deep inside me something sighs . . . first . . .
　　　　　Then sings . . . it begins a low hum
Bones pass it along. Mind has long since left!
Heart slows, slows, slows . . .
　　　　　No fear this time though.
Truth speaks: All or nothing?
What a question! Hmmm . . .

At dusk, the sky put on her shining garments
limpid blue and silver silks spun of summer thunder storms,
the kind that tease and dance in the air, twirling scarves of
    lightening
that runs along the skin of earth, but never touches or even
    lingers
long.
They hang there and then, the tenseness leaves the air
and all that's left is longing
and you weep because it never rained.

Days of blasphemy, hideously spit out of a never to be
  again benign sky
Dawn's hope suffocated in horror.
A requiem but no peace, no hope of serenity.
Shock waves quivering across the land, shattering the
  horizon,
Blind the eye, blowing airs as deadly as another original sin,
Pure unmitigated evil cold deciding, if for nothing else but
  economic necessity.
(Note: 2 million spent on research for the damn thing:
  bomb
unabated, sated and still defended rationally)
And now, under a looming forever we are condemned to
  search
For our forsaken humanity.
A brilliant summer morning that severed even bird song
  instantaneously,
Stopped prayers and brought the medieval flames of hell to
  earth
With ferocious immediacy.
Twilight darkness wrenched out of time
Stopping precisely whatever life once was or ever could be.
Skeletons with shredded skin search futilely for water to
  still their fiery thirsts.
Infernos spring up, erasing Dante's rings, writing a requiem
  that will only be
Screamed or sung by silent penitents atoning forever and
  forever, never Amen.
Never. O God, where did humankind learn such hostility?
  Such hate
Without sanity, without satiety.
(Note: this isn't poetry, or if it is, it's made of seared and
  evil memory)
Now every breath could, realistically, be our last
And the spirit that blows where it will has been sinned
  against grievously.
          —*August 6, 9, 1945; Hiroshima, Nagasaki (August 1997)*

Winter came, invading for a whole single day and night,
    exploding into May.
Snow, wind, ice dashing spring hopes, burying blooms, new
    growth, tulips' colors.
Even lambs; new born and sheep stranded in the fields
    flounder.
Three pairs of socks in my sandals, another three layers
    around shoulders,
body scrunched inside a borrowed coat. The trees all lean
    and are thrashing
heavily in the wild every which way winds. Hot tea cupped
    in cold hands,
reddened cheeks, numb nose, sipping memories of past
    months crowding in
and swirling all around. All hibernation's dreams coming
    out, bears rearing up
on hind legs, heads high, towering, bellowing, roaring and
    hungry, furiously hungry.
The taste of cake and earth mingled with mint, confusion,
    delirium. Winter came
invading for a whole single day the thirteenth of May.
After daffodils, eastering, skin crawling out to sit in the sun,
    after melting and
bursting open, taking off the clothes that guard, the
    weather reversed and catapulted
backwards to cold fragrances, being shoed unceremoniously
    back into a cocoon
Everything—taken back, assumptions denied, confronted
    brutally and humbled
subservient to weather. All arrogance defeated by ices and
    air. Restlessness
reintroduced from recesses of wind. Twilight at ten p.m.
    Crawl into the cradle of
warm quiet—tomorrow spring will leap back again and a
    great question arises—
will resurrection come again too? I know we need mercy
    and glory again.
Ah, this madness is maddeningly marvelous.

                                                    —*Scotland*

Deep-set eyes for reflection
elongated nose for breathing in the Spirit
high, broad brow for prayer
small mouth for obedience
ritual ways to paint, fast, order one's life, always
facing the doorway, the entrance in and up,
the one-way street to God. These are icon essentials.
Add in tenderness and sorrow's colors
the yearning is complete. The painting begins
its work of catching the passerby and drawing them
inside the eyes. Then it speaks and the painter
disappears gladly.

———————— ✸ ————————

pale purple tulips
lavender towards the center
edged with bruised blood
thick leaves curling up
inside themselves
lush black stamens
falling and scattering seeds
they've been indoors too long
but still they live
shriveled, a week old
ancient as flowers go
and exquisite with age
pure as old is
I think I'd like to age this way.
                        —*San Francisco*

What is home for me? the name, phrase: "I'm home!"
I'd climb trees, crawl under heavy blossomed lilac bushes,
hide behind stacks of books in the basement,
walk the boardwalk in Far Rockaway before anyone else got
up,
lie on the ground and count the stars as they come out—my
real friends.
Slip into an incense-smelling shadowed church, anywhere,
almost any one, it was old.
Cut through folks' backyards on my morning run to a half-
hour Mass, anonymous—
that was forty years ago.
A book could become four walls or desert or "limberlost"
woods, a place behind doors.
Now, a walk around Enchanted Rock, 8 or more miles
enclosing space and time,
a visit to underground trails, caverns, 140-million-year
journey back home,
a washed-out gully off the beaten trail in a park to catch
sight of the near-tamed deer,
a blank page beckoning—make home here.
I always respond. Always.

Shadows arrive early, taking the colors by the arm and
    whirling them away in scarves
chrysanthemums bloom russet, yellowy, mauve, white
    bright, falling flowers, dusty leaves.
Corn gone, just standing stalks and morning glories twined
    about. Sun-washed-out Texas sky.
In New Mexico, up north, the sage has flowered all tiny
    purple stars, the smell thick and clean.
I used to carry brown grocery sacks and cutters everywhere
    and harvest it roadside in clumps.
It stayed on my hands, pressed often to my face. I rubbed
    it in clothes, hung it from ceilings
and door jambs to dry and diffuse.
Sun falters
and the crows grow cheeky, their tribe swells.
The onset of autumn, the rituals return, time to turn and
    set face towards harvest
And memory, pick cedar and light fire. The air trembles,
    the light weakens.
It is time to pick up September's ways and start other
    dreams in motion.
Small spirits need to gather together. The dark comes on.
    Collect stones
with sun's eyes still in them along with crow's collection of
    bright strings and glass.

(continued)

Leaves fall singularly, still unnoticed, just here and there.
    Find a way to join the line dance,
just slip in. Is it summer's fringe or fall's edge?
In between is always for mourning sorrows collected and
    intimations of new patterns,
one bead at a time, begin to string them again.
This morning is a rest stop, regroup, take bearings, look at
    the map one more time,
turn onto the highway, shift season, play at being coyote,
    howl and then fix up a place
to hide in after playing. Follow owl's lead and build a new
    nest. Prepare. It is good
and necessary, right timing. Home calls back while still
    warm sun walks across the yard.
Autumn surges inside my bones and twines around my
    spirit. I stand with the corn
dry in the field.

I feel like whimpering, like a lost child, a lost soul.
　　We are thieves on either side of God in our flesh,
　　　　Dying side by side, rent by torture, breath
　　　　　　rasping,
　　Death rattling in lungs, flesh stinking though not as
　　　　badly as the righteous
　　Ones who pass by and point, gawking and insulting,
　　　　blaspheming
　　　　God's children, silent as the bombs fall once
　　　　　　again.
They cry: "Save yourself! If you can—see if God comes—
　　he called himself 'God's son.'"
What kind of God is this! Trying to redeem the death we
　　court and welcome inside us . . .
That last breath, that cry. Could it be the wind that will
　　blow death away.
　　　　Then silence vast and impenetrable . . . We still call
　　　　it Good Friday.

---　❋　---

Dusk . . . the gold light dusts the leaves.
the silence thickens, even the birds forget to sing.
Nothing stirs
Even I hold my breath
the pen poised above the page
It is a summons
everything hears it
it is a lure
a trapdoor, a threshold
I will to step over it
but I was stunned in that instant
or did I falter and look away?
Now it is night.

September Day Sit

Sitting at dusk
Coyotes start
      Yipping and howling
Back and forth across the valley.
My mind follows
Breath in and out across the sky.
      Everyone knows
Day is far along. Time to be home.
Call everyone in. Settle down.
Just this. Nothing more.
Nothing else is needed.
No / thing. Even moon comes out
      Bright, wide smile
Grinning over all, over nothing at all.
Nothing is remiss.
      God just sits, pleased
Nothing could be better than this.
Nothing at all.
      Stay. Sit still.
      Smile.
Sitting in the dark.
Still.

TRINITY WEEK

Trees dance with leaves heavy and wet
dripping, dripping blessing
baptizing. Remnants of last night's rain.
Speaking softly softly of presences
Slipping slipping through these freshest of airs.
    No moon yet tho it will rise hiding hiding
    behind the thick low hanging clouds
    lending faint light to mystery
    singing singing in singular drops
    of water kissing kissing any
    who slip through these quietest of woods.
Father breathing breathing
Son sighing sighing
Spirit falling falling
The trees waiting waiting to prey
upon all who would pass by.
Drenching in ecstasy so quiet
my heart is beating beating
in rhythm to my weeping weeping
—all for pure pleasure at the end of May.

My sole obligation is to stay, stay.

        —All Hallows, Dublin

Here the early morning belongs to the magpies
dancing on the manicured lawns
the grass all to themselves. Tails twitching.
A great expanse—but it seems they can't even get along
with no one else to interfere.
Air is cool and grey, only bits of blue and they are high
and often hidden by the scuddle of thicker air.
The high-pitched squawks intrude on any reverie.
It's only 5:30 a.m. I turn from the window ledge and
curl again into the old warmth. And bless morning
in all its grey glory.

—All Hallows, Dublin

PRAYER

I sit and squirm and try to stay still and count the minutes.
My feet go to sleep. My back aches. The ends of my fingers
    tingle.
Nonetheless the volcano bursts and hot lava moves down
the mountain and takes over everything in its path—
But it too departs from the norm—it does not set out to
    destroy
or swallow up, it lays down a loam, a layer of sediment lush
    and
life-giving and transforms the sewer sludge into fertile
    ground.
How it pulls off this fantastic feat—I am at a loss to explain.
    But
I know if I don't try to pray but just sit there, even
    grousing . . .
all hell does break loose and the sewers back up and what
    spews forth
is deadly. So I sit and count breaths before the Emptiness
and hang on for a dearer life.

                        —at the monastery

So many unmanageable impulses, memories, shocks to my
     system.
Violent pieces let loose in my mind. Ping pong balls, with
     magnets
in a confined space, a riot of noise, confusion, movement.
Am exhausted always. Even my body abruptly shuts down.
All from traveling, visiting other countries, being the
     stranger,
the outsider, rarely the guest. And so much of that other
     world
I stumbled into hurts. I hurt now, knowing.
My old world has been attacked at its roots.
Now they are bitter roots and I am estranged from myself
and where I've lived so long.

It wasn't just India—but India with its one billion people
overwhelmed concepts with immediacy, with the scale of
     violence,
with misery, with horror and grim reality. The extremes,
     even of weather,
was the norm. Evil's touch squatted in every street and
     shadowed me
in thousands of eyes, outstretched grubbing hands, severed
     limbs,
scarred bodies—it broke something inside me and left me
     bereft
of any prayer but "Mercy, God! Why?" Sigh. Cry.
I carried it home with me. They clamor inside.
They live here now.
They seek acceptance. I seek absolution—unaware of them
     so long.
May we all be one in Mercy's arms. Amen.

I REALIZE

I keep looking for a new way, a new voice
Oh, one that carries old echoes, but is reconfigured anew.
So imaginative, daring, a twist—that it seems radical—
To have come out of nowhere fully formed.
A child born without pregnancy.

It's the kind of wisdom hidden in silence
in the unsayable, in the horrific and glorious alike.
It's the kind of knowledge found in bird song
as it trills and then stops and you wait there
with bird on branch before flying off—or falling free.

It's caught in the laughter of women getting old
and loving it in some moments and others
laughing hard to keep from crying or just laying
down and dying.
But I can't get a grip on it, illusive.
I wonder if it knows and plays too?
Perhaps it is not time yet . . .

—Amsterdam

BRUSH DANCE

Purposeful, we head downhill to the bus
Engrossed in conversation—startled by singing!
But this is no bird! This is a man, a migrant worker,
an alien-outsider painting a high iron fence—consciously
with a brush and a song and the concentrated dignity
of an unself-conscious Zen master.
I am stupefied. It is the first such burst of spontaneous
     goodness
I have encountered in two long weeks in Singapore!
He saw us though there was no acknowledgment—
Humanity had scored a direct hit—a home run
In spite of pressure, and demands to produce.
I danced-walked on that strange undeciphered ground,
unknown source of that song all day long
and wished I'd stopped to gaze in appreciation of such
     freedom
shared so wildly. And more, wished I had thanked him . . .
In my delight, I never for a moment thought of it . . . sigh.

White is austere.
Bitter wind tears camellia petals off.
Bone white branches are lined in snow.
Sky scribblings white on grey.
Clarity eye blinding, heart-clearing.
Spring stirs beneath—
Yesterday I bent over plum blossoms
daring to open early.
Azure points of sky intensify
Against such brightness.
The world blazes white.
This is the knife of grief and delight.
It cannot last.
It is so lovely.
I am so alone.
It is so good.
It is separate form all but truth.
Spirit's edge. Close. So close.

—*Kyoto, Japan*

Fitful sleep, another borrowed bed, altitude acclimation.
Awakened—moonlight fills my one room house, invading
every corner and crevice, two three days shy of full!
My pillow wet with tears—
how moonlight effortlessly loves the world,
imparting radiance on all it regards
without a speck of regret.
I sit up the rest of the night apprenticed
to such endless ease of compassion.
I vow to live my life holding the world so carefully,
so recklessly, so close to the heart,
flinging abroad such ordinary joy—-
Who could refuse such a vocation?
I would lose all to dispel the violence and grief
of the world—and to bestow dignity on all that aches
and hurts. Renounce it all—just to be
a glimmer of God—to be just a wordless enclosure
a blessing every night upon the world.

VOW

I vow
to atone in my own life for all the deaths unnecessary and
    violent
for those deemed expendable.
When life is cheap, their lives go first.
Millions of children in Iraq, India, Iran, Israel, Ireland,
    Indonesia
(the litany of places that begin with I) but the world utters
this kind of killing in every place. Latest: East Timor.

I vow
to speak up, to speak out, on their behalf
for all the ones who suffer in silence, die anonymous, not
    missed,
who took their own lives in despair and lost from any
    human's care.

I vow
never to instill fear, to illicit or use language, silence or
    circumstance
let alone power against another or to aggravate any
    situation.
To approach what is volatile with Isaiah's description of the
    servant of Yahweh
who suffers—not crying out in the streets, not bruising the
    smoldering wick,
not leaning against the bruised reed, lest it break—

I vow
to beg entrance and acceptance of the stranger, the other
    who I now know
not as just my neighbor to be loved as I love myself
    but as sacrament of
the Incarnation to be tendered as God tends to me.

(continued)

I vow
to salvage the poor, the ignored, the despised and
    diminished
and kiss them over and over again like mothers kiss away
their children's hurts, scratches, bruises and bumps, while
    wiping their
smudged and tear-stained frightened faces—
and steadfastly refuse to stop until they collapse in laughter
or giddiness or delight. Why not?
Everyone was created for small glories and daily dignity.

I vow
to search out and adamantly stake every day on the
    unforeseen,
the stranger come, the absolutely impossible, the
    miraculous,
the gestures of grace, the silent screaming of the Spirit
    trying
to distract us from the banal and to proudly and quietly
    repeat:
"This is the day the Lord has made, let us be glad and
    rejoice in it!"
To practice resurrection, if need be, with a vengeance and
    a passion
heretofore reserved for making love.

I vow
to be gloriously attached to life, to being human, even the
    hardscrabble
Gut-wrenching and groaning parts, the catastrophes—as
    well as the
Stunning and deliciously sweet pieces.

(continued)

I vow
to praise in words and write ceaselessly, but I will only let
what has been birthed in silences, water and blood be
    spoken
in my worship and truthtelling.

I vow
to stand witness and not let the extremities people are made
to endure pass by unheeded. I will protest and give vent to
lamentation. I will be a question mark and an exclamation
    point.
Mantra-like whispering and shouting, chanting No! It is not
    allowed!
No more! Enough! Desist! Stop! Don't buckle under or close
    your eyes
or turn away! See! Look! Contemplate and declare!

I vow
to believe in non-violent resistance to all that dehumanizes,
to all that undermines hope and all that sucks the life-blood
    of justice
from another. Along with the stars of night I will stand
    witness
and remember all those nameless who once watched the
    night sky
and dreamed of kindness and of peace on earth.

I vow
austerity, not the grim and artless kind that decries beauty
and the goodness of all that is made and given over to us to
    share
but the kind that is founded on appreciation, the deeply
    embedded debt
of sheer gratitude.

(continued)

I vow
to savor, finger, run my heart over and impart spirit to all
that languishes, strip excess to quicken another's failing
    strength,
learn the bare necessities I need so others can know less
    need.
I will limit desire and channel even my anger into life-lines
for those slipping away unnoticed and stave off sorrow.
No grasping. Instead laughing.

I vow
to court insecurity that can be remedied by sharing
and community, even reveling in the poor's generosity.
But I will be profligate with hope and all it takes
to set the prisoners free.

I vow
to be pure and live with integrity. I will!

Written, remembering a line: "In such a world, justice is
    a continent
always being discovered by taking soundings."
    (Wm. Stafford)
These are my soundings late December 1999
I will not relent from living. Not ever! Amen.